Young Voices Unheard: Children's Views from Scotland and Greece on Education

Authored by

Evanthia Synodi
*Department of Preschool Education
University of Crete
Gallos Campus
Rethymno, 74100,
Greece*

Young Voices Unheard: Children's Views from Scotland and Greece on Education

Author: Evanthia Synodi

ISBN (Online): 978-981-5124-66-8

ISBN (Print): 978-981-5124-67-5

ISBN (Paperback): 978-981-5124-68-2

© 2023, Bentham Books imprint.

Published by Bentham Science Publishers Pte. Ltd. Singapore. All Rights Reserved.

First published in 2023.

BENTHAM SCIENCE PUBLISHERS LTD.
End User License Agreement (for non-institutional, personal use)

This is an agreement between you and Bentham Science Publishers Ltd. Please read this License Agreement carefully before using the ebook/echapter/ejournal (**"Work"**). Your use of the Work constitutes your agreement to the terms and conditions set forth in this License Agreement. If you do not agree to these terms and conditions then you should not use the Work.

Bentham Science Publishers agrees to grant you a non-exclusive, non-transferable limited license to use the Work subject to and in accordance with the following terms and conditions. This License Agreement is for non-library, personal use only. For a library / institutional / multi user license in respect of the Work, please contact: permission@benthamscience.net.

Usage Rules:

1. All rights reserved: The Work is the subject of copyright and Bentham Science Publishers either owns the Work (and the copyright in it) or is licensed to distribute the Work. You shall not copy, reproduce, modify, remove, delete, augment, add to, publish, transmit, sell, resell, create derivative works from, or in any way exploit the Work or make the Work available for others to do any of the same, in any form or by any means, in whole or in part, in each case without the prior written permission of Bentham Science Publishers, unless stated otherwise in this License Agreement.
2. You may download a copy of the Work on one occasion to one personal computer (including tablet, laptop, desktop, or other such devices). You may make one back-up copy of the Work to avoid losing it.
3. The unauthorised use or distribution of copyrighted or other proprietary content is illegal and could subject you to liability for substantial money damages. You will be liable for any damage resulting from your misuse of the Work or any violation of this License Agreement, including any infringement by you of copyrights or proprietary rights.

Disclaimer:

Bentham Science Publishers does not guarantee that the information in the Work is error-free, or warrant that it will meet your requirements or that access to the Work will be uninterrupted or error-free. The Work is provided "as is" without warranty of any kind, either express or implied or statutory, including, without limitation, implied warranties of merchantability and fitness for a particular purpose. The entire risk as to the results and performance of the Work is assumed by you. No responsibility is assumed by Bentham Science Publishers, its staff, editors and/or authors for any injury and/or damage to persons or property as a matter of products liability, negligence or otherwise, or from any use or operation of any methods, products instruction, advertisements or ideas contained in the Work.

Limitation of Liability:

In no event will Bentham Science Publishers, its staff, editors and/or authors, be liable for any damages, including, without limitation, special, incidental and/or consequential damages and/or damages for lost data and/or profits arising out of (whether directly or indirectly) the use or inability to use the Work. The entire liability of Bentham Science Publishers shall be limited to the amount actually paid by you for the Work.

General:

1. Any dispute or claim arising out of or in connection with this License Agreement or the Work (including non-contractual disputes or claims) will be governed by and construed in accordance with the laws of Singapore. Each party agrees that the courts of the state of Singapore shall have exclusive jurisdiction to settle any dispute or claim arising out of or in connection with this License Agreement or the Work (including non-contractual disputes or claims).
2. Your rights under this License Agreement will automatically terminate without notice and without the

need for a court order if at any point you breach any terms of this License Agreement. In no event will any delay or failure by Bentham Science Publishers in enforcing your compliance with this License Agreement constitute a waiver of any of its rights.

3. You acknowledge that you have read this License Agreement, and agree to be bound by its terms and conditions. To the extent that any other terms and conditions presented on any website of Bentham Science Publishers conflict with, or are inconsistent with, the terms and conditions set out in this License Agreement, you acknowledge that the terms and conditions set out in this License Agreement shall prevail.

Bentham Science Publishers Pte. Ltd.
80 Robinson Road #02-00
Singapore 068898
Singapore
Email: subscriptions@benthamscience.net

CONTENTS

PREFACE	i

THEORETICAL PART

CHAPTER 1 THE CONVENTION ON THE RIGHTS OF THE CHILD	1
INTRODUCTION	1
Explanatory Documents	4
General Comment No 7 (2005): Implementing Child Rights in Early Childhood	4
General Comment No. 1 (2001), Article 29 (1): The Aims of Education	6
General Comment No. 12 (2009): The right of the Child to be Heard	7
General Comment No. 14 (2013) on the Right of the Child to have his or her Best Interests taken as a Primary Consideration (art.3, para. 1)	8
Interpretations of Children's Rights	8
CHAPTER 2 MODELS OF SCHOOLING AND CHILDREN'S RIGHTS	12
INTRODUCTION	12
The Authoritarian School	12
The School Based on Traditional Developmental Psychology	14
The Rights Based School	15
NOTES	16

EMPIRICAL RESEARCH PART

CHAPTER 3 METHODOLOGY	17
INTRODUCTION	17
Background to the Conceptualization of this Research	18
Comparative Study	20
Qualitative Research	25
Method	26
Research Tools	27
The First Focus Group Session	27
Second Focus Group Session	32
Research Questions	33
Sample and Participants	33
Research Ethics	34
Official Permission for Research	34
Contact with Research Gatekeepers	34
Anonymity	34
Research Process	35
Power Issues	35
Ensuring the Trustworthiness of the Research	36
NOTES	40
CHAPTER 4 CHILDREN'S VIEWS ABOUT AN AUTHORITARIAN SCHOOL	42
INTRODUCTION	42
The Physical Environment of a School	43
Scotland	43
Greece	49
Comparison of Children's Perspectives on the Physical Environment	55
The Social Environment of A School	56
Scotland	56
Greece	63

Comparison of Children's Perspectives on the Social Environment	71
NOTES	72
CHAPTER 5 CHILDREN'S VIEWS ABOUT A SCHOOL BASED ON DEVELOPMENTAL PSYCHOLOGY	74
INTRODUCTION	74
The Physical Environment of A School	75
Scotland	75
Greece	81
Comparison of Children's Perspectives on the Physical Environment	89
Social Environment of A School	90
Scotland	90
Greece	97
Comparison of Children's Perspectives on the Social Environment	99
NOTES	99
CHAPTER 6 CHILDREN'S VIEWS ABOUT A RIGHTS-BASED SCHOOL	101
INTRODUCTION	101
The Physical Environment of the School	102
Scotland	102
Greece	105
Comparison of Children's Views on the Physical Environment	111
The Social Environment Of A School	112
Scotland	112
Greece	115
Comparison Of Children's Views On The Social Environment	120
NOTES	120
CHAPTER 7 THE PERFECT SCHOOL FOR WILSON	121
INTRODUCTION	121
Scotland	122
Valley School MX1	122
Valley School MX2	125
Hill School AU	128
Hill School DP	131
Comparison of Data within Scotland	138
Greece	139
Elm School AU	139
Elm School RB	142
Elm School MX1	147
Oak School AU	149
Oak School DP	152
Oak School RB	154
Pine School AU	158
Pine School MX	161
Comparison of Data Within Greece	168
Comparison of Data From Scotland And Greece	169
NOTES	171
CHAPTER 8 CONCLUSIONS	173
INTRODUCTION	173
Methodology of Research	174
Main Findings of the First Focus Group Sessions	176

  The Physical Environment of a School and Children's Rights 176
  The Social Environment Of a School and Children's Rights 178
 Main Findings of the Second Focus Group Sessions 180
  The Perfect School for Wilson 180
 Findings and the Convention on the Rights of the Child 181
 Findings and the Conceptualizations of Schooling 183
 Children's Rights, School and Play 185
 Implications of the Study 188
 Further Research on the Topic 188
NOTES 189
REFERENCES 190
SUBJECT INDEX 200

PREFACE

This book is dedicated to some young children's views on a variety of aspects of school provision and school practices that have been in place or advocated for young children. I related these provisions to children's rights in terms of whether they indicate respect to or violation of children's rights. Then, children's views and preferences on school provisions and practices are discussed in connection with the children's rights as defined in the Convention on the Rights of a Child (United Nations [UN], 1989). This way it was ascertained which educational provisions and practices young children prioritized and consequently which rights they favored or not.

What is it about?

I undertook this study because I wanted to record the views of children aged five to six years in Greece and Scotland on three different types of school provision and practice arranged for young children over the years. The three different models of schooling selected for children to discuss were analyzed in order to show which of the children's rights pertaining to their education they reflected and which they violated. The first model of schooling is the teacher-centered school, which shows no respect for children's rights except perhaps partly their right to education (article 28.1 of the Convention). This is how I shall refer to the Convention on the rights of the child (United Nations, 1989) henceforth). The next school model is based on traditional developmental psychology and it allows adults the scope and potential to respect some of the children's rights, such as play (article 31), but neglects or ignores others, such as freedom of conscience or religion (articles 14 & 30). The last model of school is the rights-based school, which fully respects all children's rights pertaining to their attending school.

The special contribution of such a study is that it reveals some young children's voices in multiple ways. First, young children were given the opportunity to discuss specific education practices, which have been implemented over time in early year's classes. This way I was able to produce data on the same topics but from children living in two different countries, national cultures and education provision. These children also had the opportunity to describe their ideal school for a child of their age, in the form of suggestions for establishing a school for Wilson, who did not want to go to school. In this case too, the children who offered their ideas came from Scotland and Greece and from different cultures and schooling. Subsequently, this data, e.g. children's suggestions, thoughts, and ideas, is related to their rights so as to show which ones the participants themselves prioritized. The differences in priorities were explained based on children's experience of schooling and their national cultures.

Why Children's Rights?

Greece ratified the Convention on the rights of the child in 1992, whereas the UK, part of which is Scotland, in 1991. As a result, legislation pertaining to children in both countries is to conform to what is foreseen by the Convention. Some of the rights children have, according to the Convention, are not so easy to inform changes in the existing legislation due to the varieties of cultural perspectives of citizens in both countries on childhood, children, and their rights. For example, both countries have a mandatory curriculum, which means that some of its aspects, such as the goals of learning that children must achieve, cannot be negotiated or omitted to suit children's interests or choices in accordance with article 12 of the Convention.

This phenomenon is recorded in many countries, since their cultures are in juxtaposition with some of the children's rights in the Convention, especially those of child participation (Frost, 2011, as cited in Jones & Walker, 2011, p. 53; Kanyal & Gibbs, 2014; UN General Comment 7, 2005; Welsh, 2008, as cited in Jones & Walker, 2011). Many adults, regardless of their background, hold different perspectives on childhood and the immaturity that characterizes young human beings from the perspective on which the Convention is based (e.g. Cunningham, 2005, 2006). Therefore, some adults think that children lack maturity, abilities, and reason in absolute terms, so they treat them with less respect and dismiss them and their views (Archard, 2004; Cunningham, 2005). However, according to the Convention, adults, including teachers and parents, have the responsibility of giving children direction and guidance in relation to exercising their rights (article 5 of the Convention). This means that adults must help children find the place they are entitled in society, rather than allow the dominant culture in any society to give children a predetermined position, which may not always correspond to all children's potential.

Why Young Children?

Children need to be given a voice, to be able to have a say in the provision adults make for their education. This is something I believe in and is in accordance with article 12 of the Convention. Article 12 defines children's right to express their 'views freely in all matters affecting the child, the views of the child being given due weight in accordance with the age and maturity of the child'.

As Allison James (2007, p. 262) explains, however, 'giving voice to children is not simply or only about letting children speak: it is about exploring the unique contribution to our understanding of and theorizing about the social world [part of which is school] that children's perspectives can provide'. This is even more true for younger children for whom the provision and protection rights tend to be favored by adults over their participation rights. Young children are considered immature by many people and thus their opinions are not valued or sought (Archard, 2004). This has led the United Nations to issue General Comment No. 7 (2005) on early childhood to clarify that all children regardless of their age have all the rights foreseen by the Convention.

Why these countries?

Greece and Scotland have certain features, which enable a meaningful comparison (Clarkson, 2009). These countries offer different educational provisions to children aged five to six years both in terms of the type of school (preschool education in Greece and primary education in Scotland) and of financial aid to schools (Scotland devotes a larger part of its budget to education than Greece[1] does). The dominant cultural perceptions of children's and people's rights are also different, if not opposite, in these two countries. Children in Scotland are taught to be independent of the beginning of their lives, whereas in Greece, the children's environment in family and school is overprotective and collectivist (e.g. Farlane, 2018).

On the other hand, both countries have populations mainly Christian, White and European, which means that they share some common ideas about childhood and young children's education. Therefore, there exists a fruitful balance of similarities and differences between Scotland and Greece to justify their selection for a study in Comparative Early Childhood Education.

How was the research conducted?

Apart from this study being comparative in nature, it is also qualitative with data produced through focus group sessions with young children. The novelty of this research, on top of it is a comparative one, is that its participants are young children aged 5 to 6 years and that its method of data production is focus group; a not so usual way of researching on children (Gibson, 2007).

What is the value of this study?

As an educator I think five to six year old children in schools can be offered more opportunities to learn (a) what their rights are according to the Convention, which both Scotland and Greece have ratified, and (b) how to act as right holders. In accordance with articles 5 and 29 of the Convention, people who are responsible for children, which includes teachers, have the responsibility to teach them about their rights and facilitate them in exercising them.

With this study adults involved in young children's education gain insight into the matter of how children feel about certain practices and provisions. Such insight can be considered when defining and determining good practices in schools for five-year-old children in Greece and Scotland in general. This insight is also valuable when considering how teachers can better cater to article 5 of the Convention, especially at the initial teacher education level. Furthermore, in an age of education leadership, regardless of whether it refers to headteachers / principals or teachers themselves (Leithwood, 1992; Leithwood, Harris, & Hopkins, 2008; Smylie & Eckert, 2018), such studies can contribute to the improvement of young children's education and to a school life respectful of children's rights.

What is the structure of this book?

In the first chapter of this book, the Convention is presented. Particular consideration is given to the rights that apply to children's education in school together with the relevant to children's education General Comments (General Comment 7, 2005; General Comment 1, 2001; General Comment 12, 2009 and General Comment 14, 2013) issued by the United Nations. These documents are selected because they are what Scotland and Greece committed to abide by in relation to the educational provision for their young children.

The second chapter is about the models of education that are known and have been partly or full implemented in the Western world. The models are embodied in the authoritarian school, the school based on traditional developmental psychology and the rights-based school. These models of schooling for young children are related to the rights foreseen by the Convention for the children in order to determine which rights they respect and facilitate and which they violate. Aspects of these models were discussed by the children who participated in this study. The next chapter is dedicated to the methodology of the research undertaken. 56 children from Scotland and Greece participated in two focus group sessions in groups of 4. In the first session, children discussed three models of education that have been advocated for them. I chose some of the features of each of the three conceptualizations of school and made them features of three plans for the best school ever, which children discussed. In a second session with each group, children were read the beginning of the book *Whiffy Wilson: The wolf who wouldn't go to school* and asked to describe the features of a school that would make Wilson want to attend. Both of these sessions were followed by children drawing aspects of what they discussed.

iv

In the empirical part of the study, the data are analyzed in four chapters. In the first chapter of the second one, the data about the plan for a school based on traditional developmental psychology. In the third chapter, children's views on the plan for a rights-based school are analyzed whereas in the fourth chapter, the data about a perfect school for Wilson. The analysis of the data from both focus group sessions showed that children prioritized children's right to play, safety, consultation and education. In the final chapter of this study, the conclusions of the study are presented together with recommendations for further research.

Note:

Even though Greece has double the population of Scotland for the year 2022, for example, Greece allocated 4.943.012£ (5.841.100 €) to education and Scotland 4.207.700£ according to their official budget sites. (Hellenic Republic, 2021 and Scottish Government, 2021).

Evanthia Synodi
Department of Preschool Education
University of Crete
Gallos Campus
Rethymno, 74100,
Greece

THEORETICAL PART

In this part of the study, its theoretical underpinnings are analyzed in two chapters. In the first chapter, the rights of children entitled according to international legislation are analyzed as well as how their implementation changes the power balance in the relationship between adults and children. In the second chapter, three conceptualizations of education for children are examined in relation to whether they respect, promote and facilitate the implementation of children's rights. These three models of schooling are the teacher-centered, the traditional developmental psychology based and the rights-based, which children discussed in the empirical part of this study.

CHAPTER 1

The Convention on the Rights of the Child

Abstract: In this chapter, children's rights as defined by the Convention on the rights of the child are analyzed, since the Convention has been ratified by Scotland and Greece. According to the Convention, children have protection, provision, and participation rights. Some of the General Comments issued by the United Nations on children's rights are discussed as they are related to young children's education. It is evident that participation rights are more difficult to implement, as they imply more power for the children and acknowledgement of their competency.

Keywords: Convention on the rights of the child, General Comments, Greece, Participation rights, Protection rights, Provision rights, Scotland.

INTRODUCTION

In this chapter, the rights of children according to the Convention and other relevant documents by the United Nations are presented and analyzed. However, before discussing the literature on children's rights, the definition of rights must be clarified. A right 'is something you should always be able to do, to have, to know, to say or to be protected from', according to Jones (2011a, p. 4). However, one must not forget that rights come with responsibilities, which are 'something you should do for other people, for society or for the environment' (Jones, 2011a, p. 4).

The Convention on the Rights of the Child (United Nations [UN], 1989) foresees rights for all children that must be respected and implemented by every country, which has ratified the Convention. These rights have been grouped in various ways. The International Save the Children Alliance (2007), for example, discusses children's rights in terms of the four general principles of the Convention:

1. Article 2 and children's right not to be discriminated.

2. Article 3 and children's right to their best interest being the primary concern in all actions concerning children.

3. Article 6 and children's right to live and develop.

4. Article 12 and children's right to participation in all matters affecting them and their right to be heard (International Save the Children Alliance, 2007).

Jones and Welch (2018) categorize the rights defined in the Convention into liberty rights and welfare rights of children. Liberty rights are based on the notion that people have the right to live and act freely, to be free and to look out for their interests. In such a case, the state intervenes only 'with the will of the people' (Jones & Welch, 2018, p. 42). Each individual is considered to be autonomous and responsible for themselves, their family and their property. However, not all people have the same start in life or equal capacities, therefore, they cannot make a good life for themselves and their families. This means that there must be some provision in place so as to help everybody 'make the best use of their liberty rights' (Jones & Welch, 2018, p. 44). This provision is made available by the state in the form of welfare rights, such as healthcare and education (Jones & Welch, 2018).

Others, such as Te One (2011) and Alderson (2008), group the rights of the Convention into three categories. According to them, the Convention includes rights of protection, provision and participation for all children and clarifies that all types of rights should be implemented in combination and not in isolation (UN, 1989, Preamble; General Comment 7, 2005, article 3; Te One, 2011).

The protection rights children are entitled to are the right of children to be protected from any kind of discrimination (article 2), children's right to have adults act in the children's best interest (article 3), the right to be protected from any kind of abuse (articles 19, 33 and 34), to be protected from exploitation (articles 32, 35, and 36), to be protected from injustice (article 40) and from war dangers (article 38) (Alderson, 2008; Archard, 2004; Te One, 2011).

The rights regarding the quality of family life children are entitled (articles 5, 18 and 27), children's right to health, safety and education (articles 24, 26 and 28), children's right to provision for their general development in education (article 29), for their physical and special care (articles 6 and 23) and for play, spare time, fun and children's culture (article 31) are considered to be provision rights for children (Alderson, 2008; Archard, 2004; Te One, 2011).

The participation rights that children are entitled to are children's right to their identity (articles 7, 8 and 30), their right to be consulted, and their views considered in accordance with their age and maturity when decisions about their lives are made (article 12), their right to access information (article 17), children's right to freedom of speech, expression and thought (articles 13 and 14) and their right to a private life (article 16) (Alderson, 2008; Archard, 2004; Te One, 2011).

Even though all rights apply to all children at all times and are interconnected, some of the articles of the Convention are clearly related to education and how schools should operate. These articles are:

1. Article 2, which states that children are not to be discriminated against for any reason. The grounds for discrimination forbidden by the Convention are children's or their parent's / guardian's 'race, color, sex, language, religion, political opinion, national, ethnic, or social origin, property, disability, birth or other status'.

2. Article 3, which states that in all actions concerning children (some of which are related to their education) the best interests of the child should be a primary consideration.

3. Article 5, which defines that people legally responsible for a child, who include their teachers, need to provide them with guidance and direction in the exercise of their rights.

4. Article 13 and children's right to freedom of expression. This includes schools where children seek, receive and impart information and ideas in ways they choose, except if they are against the law or violate other people's respective rights.

5. Article 14, which states that the child's right to freedom of 'thought, conscience and religion' shall be respected, except if it is against the law or violates other people's respective rights. This kind of respect is expected, therefore, by schools and teachers.

6. Article 23, which refers to the right to an effective access to education and to providing education for the mentally or physically disabled children. Such education should ensure their dignity, self-reliance and their active participation in society, part of which is a school.

7. Article 24, which refers to children's right to education on health issues, hygiene and prevention of accidents.

8. Article 28, which refers to all children's right to education. Primary education must be compulsory for all, whereas all types of secondary education must be developed and available to all children free of charge. Measures must be taken to minimize the number of children dropping out of school as well as to provide education 'on the basis of equal opportunities' (article 28.1). School discipline is linked to respecting children's dignity and all of their rights included in the Convention.

9. Article 29, which further explains the type of education children are entitled. Children have a right to an education that develops their 'personality, talents' and potential, cultivates their 'respect (a) for human rights' and freedoms, (b) for their parents, for their cultural identities, 'language and values', (c) for the 'national values' of their country of origin and of residence and (d) for other 'civilizations'. Such education also teaches children to respect the natural environment and to lead a responsible life, when they are adults, with understanding, tolerance and friendship and without discrimination towards others either in their country or in other places of the world.

10. Article 30, which refers to the children of ethnic, religious or linguistic minorities in any country. These children have the right to enjoy their 'language, culture and religion in community with other members of their group', which applies to school, as well as other institutions children with such background may find themselves.

11. Article 31, which refers to children's right to play, leisure, recreational, cultural and artistic activities. These types of activities form part of school life too, and not only of children's social and family life.

12. Children's protection from any kind of physical and mental harm (article 19) also applies to schools. Schools must protect children from economic exploitation (article 32) and substance abuse (article 33).

13. As protection from sexual exploitation (article 34) or other harms that may come to children (article 36) are children's rights, too, schools have an obligation to uphold these rights.

Explanatory Documents

The need for clarification on children's rights in general and in relation to school led to the issuing of General Comments by the United Nations, four of which are relevant to this study.

General Comment No 7 (2005): Implementing Child Rights in Early Childhood

The United Nations published General Comment number 7 (UN Committee on the Rights of the Child, 2005, henceforth GC 7, 2005) regarding children from birth to the age of 8 years (GC 7, 2005, article 4). This age range includes children aged five to six years who are at the center of this study. The main message of the Comment is that younger children have the same rights the Convention declares as older children (GC 7, 2005, articles 1 and 3).

The document paints the profile of the young child, which is relevant to the staff working in schools with children, as it interferes with the respect, protection and fulfillment of children's rights in school (GC 7, 2005, articles 2 and 8). Young children, too, are persons who are to be respected, who have their interests, views and concerns and who are active members of society (GC 7, 2005, article 5). The document clarifies that early childhood is not 'a period for the socialization of the immature human being' one must go through in order to become mature and adult (GC 7, 2005, article 5).

Young children grow quickly in every aspect of development and actively learn with other children and adults about 'the physical, social and cultural' environment (GC 7, 2005, article 6(d)). What they require from their caregivers is 'nurturance, care, guidance and protection, in ways they are respectful of their individuality and growing capacities' (GC 7, 2005, article 6(b)). They make relationships with other children through which they learn and develop social and citizen skills, such as how to negotiate, share, resolve conflicts, take responsibility and strike agreements (GC 7, 2005, article 6(c)). Children's learning and development are influenced by the children's own 'nature' (GC 7, 2005, article 6(f)), their sex, family and school, health and care conditions (GC 7, 2005, article 6(f)) and beliefs about their capacities, needs and position in society (GC 7, 2005, article 6(g)). Variations in beliefs about their capacities, needs and position in society are to be respected in school, too, unless they are in disagreement with children's rights as determined in the Convention (GC 7, 2005, article 2(e) and 8).

In the General Comment 7, discrimination in early childhood is further explained. The document defines ways that discrimination against young children is expressed, which apply to schools, too (GC 7, 2005, article 11). Discrimination against children is expressed in the form of 'reduced levels of nutrition; inadequate care and attention; restricted opportunities for play, learning and education (GC 7, 2005, articles 11 and 34); inhibition of free expression of feelings and views … harsh treatment and unreasonable expectations, which may be exploitative or abusive' (GC 7, 2005, article 11). The Comment also mentions that children can be victims of multiple discrimination.

The Comment declares that all children regardless of their age are entitled to be consulted whether as individuals or as a group (GC 7, 2005, article 14). This means that the right defined in article 12 of the Convention is to be respected and implemented, even when it comes to young children. That is so, because young children are not 'undeveloped' but able to understand, communicate in a variety of ways and make choices (GC 7, 2005, article 14). The document repeats that it is the adults who need to learn how to consult children especially before children can speak or write (GC 7, 2005, article 14; see also Alderson, 2008; Jones &

Welch, 2018). It recommends their teachers (a) adopt a child-centered approach, (b) listen to children, and (c) respect their dignity and their views (GC 7, 2005, article 14(c)). The Comment shows that article 12 of the Convention also applies to education in general, and to the education of young children in particular.

Moreover, the document analyzes article 29 of the Convention and children's right to education further. Article 28 of the General Comment explains that one of the aims of preschool education is to empower children by developing their skills, learning, potential, sense of dignity and self-esteem in child-centered ways. It also defines that young children should have education as well as care with three features. This educare for young children should (a) respect all their human rights, (b) be child-centered and (c) teach children about human rights and how to respect and assert them (GC 7, 2005, article 33). Therefore, article 33 of GC 7 2005 requires that human rights become part of preschool education both as content and as practice.

Out of the four General Comments relevant to this study, this is the only one which describes children as social actors (articles 2 and 8) and as agents (articles 14 and 16) without ever defining the terms. In its articles 2 and 8, it is clarified that the purpose of GC 7 2005 is to encourage people to see children as social actors. Even though it does not define what this means, it gives details of the social actor's life. The survival, well-being and development of these social actors depend on their close relationships with other people. According to the document, young social actors also have vulnerabilities, interests and capacities and require protection, guidance and support to exercise their rights.

In its articles 14 and 16, the document characterizes young children as social agents who need protection, nurturance and understanding from their family, again, for their survival and well-being. However, these articles draw attention to how children's agency is sometimes ignored because of their age and immaturity.

According to GC 7 in general, young children, then, are capable as well as vulnerable, in need of close nurturing relationships with other people and of help to learn how to exercise their rights.

General Comment No. 1 (2001), Article 29 (1): The Aims of Education

The General Comment No. 1 (UN Committee on the Rights of the Child, 2001) adds some more clarification on the education of children in general, which by default applies to the education of young children [GC 1, 2001 henceforth]. The document clarifies that their education must promote children's enjoyment of their rights in terms of the provided curriculum, methods, educational processes and environment with particular reference to the disciplinary proceedings (GC 1, 2001, article 8).

Schools are also linked to 'the struggle against racism, racial discrimination, xenophobia' and intolerance (GC 1, 2001, article 11). They are, furthermore, perceived as institutions cultivating and actively teaching about education for peace, tolerance and respect for the natural environment (GC 1, 2001, article 13), human rights (GC 1, 2001, articles 15 and 20) and international humanitarian law and actively involving children in such learning. Schools must fight 'ignorance, unfounded fears of racial, ethnic, religious, cultural and linguistic or other forms of difference', prejudices or distorted values with 'respect for differences' and accomplish that by challenging discrimination and prejudice within the community each school caters for (GC 1, 2001, articles 11 and 19).

GC 1 2001 clarifies that a school where children experience 'excessive burden of work' and competition among them can harm children's fullest potential of their abilities (GC 1, 2001, article 12). Finally, it recommends children as well as teachers being enabled to report shortcomings (GC 1, 2001, article 22) and lodge complaints (GC 1, 2001, article 25) on how aspects of children's right to education (article 29 of the Convention) are not fulfilled at school.

General Comment No. 12 (2009): The right of the Child to be Heard

The General Comment No. 12 (UN Committee on the Rights of the Child, 2009) analyses children's right to be heard [GC 12, 2009 henceforth]. The document explains that even the youngest children hold this right defined in article 12 of the Convention and it is the adults who need to learn how to consult children (by analyzing, for example, children's glances, gestures, and language). It clarifies that article 3 of the Convention (the best interests of the child are the priority for each decision affecting their lives) and article 12 of the Convention are complimentary. According to GC 12 2009, article 12 of the Convention is related to its articles 13 about children's right to freedom of expression (GC 12, 2009, articles 68 and 80-81), to article 17 about children's right to access to information (GC 12, 2009, articles 70-74) and articles 28-29 about children's right to education (GC 12, 2009, articles 105-114). All the above rights, *i.e.* children's right to express their views freely in all matters affecting their lives (article 12 of the Convention), to freely express themselves (article 13 of the Convention) and to have access to information (article 17 of the Convention), are clearly related to all matters schools (articles 28 and 29 of the Convention) have to handle and provide for (GC 12, 2009, article 49).

General Comment No. 14 (2013) on the Right of the Child to have his or her Best Interests taken as a Primary Consideration (art.3, para. 1)

General Comment 14 (UN Committee on the Rights of the Child, 2013), refers to the best interests of the child (GC 14, 2013 henceforth). It repeats and explains the complementary relationship between article 3 and article 12 of the Convention further (GC 14, 2013, articles 43 and 89-91) and clarifies that these two articles are relevant to education (GC 14, 2013, articles 32-35 and 79). Article 3 of the Convention explains that children have the right to their best interests being the primary consideration in all actions concerning them and, in this particular document, education is distinctly included in these actions (GC 14, 2013, articles 19, 26, 30, 32, 71, 84, 94, 95).

Article 79 of this Comment undoubtedly relates article 3 of the Convention to early childhood education. According to article 79, early childhood education needs to be of quality and free of charge and provided by 'well-trained teachers', in 'a child-friendly environment' and with 'appropriate teaching and learning methods'. The purpose of early childhood education is twofold; early childhood education is an investment as well as an opportunity for 'joyful activities, respect, participation and fulfillment of ambitions'. In schools, children's best interests are ensured if children are helped to overcome their vulnerability. To overcome their vulnerability, children must be offered all the above as well as responsibilities in school.

Interpretations of Children's Rights

There exist three theses that interpret the role of adults in relation to the rights children have and to the adults' perceptions of what a child and childhood are. These thesis's are (a) the thesis of children's interests or protection, (b) the thesis of provision for the children and their rights and (c) the thesis of children's choices or children's participation (Te One, 2011).

According to the first position, children are not capable of exercising their rights and they need adults to do that for them. This position prioritizes certain rights, the protection rights of the Convention, which children have, over the rest. So, even though children are recognized as rights holders, there is still some influence of other perceptions of children such as the innocent child (Rousseau, n.d., as cited in Teasar, 2016) in need of protection from the evils and the corruption of society (Archard, 2004; Blenkin & Kelly, 1997; MacNaughton, Hughes, & Smith, 2007).

According to the provision rights thesis, children cannot exercise their rights mainly because they cannot make choices and decisions (Te One, 2011). Therefore, the provision rights are prioritized and adults decide for children (MacNaughton, Hughes & Smith, 2007). This interpretation of children's rights echoes the model of the child as deficient (Archard, 2004; Bruce, 1997), since the emphasis is on the adult whom the child will become. It is also influenced by the model of the child as an empty vessel (Locke, n.d., as cited in Tesar, 2016) who needs to be taught by adults and by the model of the child as evil (Hobbes, n.d., as cited in Tesar, 2016) who needs adults to teach them how to find their place in society.

The third position on the rights of the child, *i.e.* choice or participation thesis, is based on the rationale that adults must accept that children have the right to make choices as well as a developing capacity to make choices. Children's participation rights are based on a perception of children different from the perceptions widely known, and discussed above. They are based on the perception that children are capable to learn, to form opinions, to think for themselves and about their lives so that they have a say in them (Hedegaard, 2008; Smith, Duncan, & Marshall, 2005). Additionally, more and more indications and evidence are accumulated that children do and can do much more either at a developmental level or at exercising their rights than traditionally believed and advocated (Alderson, 2008; Hall & Kofkin Rudkin, 2011; Jones & Walker, 2011; Vasquez, 2004).

The rationale behind the perceptions of the child which prioritize the protection and provision of rights seems to maintain an imbalance in terms of power between adults and children (*e.g.* Devine, 1999). In my view, the rights of provision and protection of children are rights that do not collide with the culture of many adults nowadays (see also Jones, 2011b). Many adults want to protect children and decide what is best for them. They want children to be healthy and educated, protected from abuse, exploitation and all sorts of discrimination. These rights do not collide with the power and control adults have over children and their lives. On the contrary, they enhance the power and control adults have if children's participation rights are not taken into consideration. Children's participation rights limit the control adults have over every aspect of their lives and thus cause some adults' reactions (Te One, 2011).

Children's participation rights seem to cause a lot of problems, because some adults find it difficult to respect, protect and fulfill children's rights, in accordance with the definition of these terms by the organization International Save the Children Alliance (2007). Some adults do not acknowledge children as human beings with rights or with participation rights in particular, which they do not respect. Not all adults can protect children from other people who do not respect children's rights, therefore, children's participation rights are not always protected. Finally, many adults do not help children learn about their rights and how to assert them, so children do not fulfill their participation rights.

One of these participation rights is children's right to express their views and for them to be heard when decisions are made which affect children's lives (UN, 1989, article 12). Some adults do not consult the children they are responsible for. Others do not use or are hindered from using their consultations with children, as the steps of a variety of participation theories exemplify (Arnstein, 1969; Cornwall, 2008; Francis & Lorenzo, 2002; Kanyal, 2014; Percy-Smith, 2010). Even if they are aware of and respect children's right to be consulted, a lot of people cannot balance its importance with that of article 3 of the Convention (Archard & Skivenes, 2009) and the responsibility of adults to do the best for children. This is problematic for many people of all cultures, western or not, as various authors have shown (*e.g.* Alderson, 2008; Archard, 2004; Kaime, 2011).

Teachers themselves are some of the adults who find it challenging and problematic to allow children to exercise all of their rights at school or for themselves to implement and respect children's rights at work. Children's right to tell their opinion and for their opinion to be seriously considered when forming any decision or policy for children seems to create some problems when it comes to their education. Their right not to be discriminated against is not respected many times by adults in school, because of children's young age, which is linked to immaturity and its negative connotations and not necessarily because of proof of children's incapacity to form opinions or make decisions. The above can cause problems with young children's education because the adults involved in children's lives, education and care may have a perspective on matters different from the children's.

State-run education, if not education in general, aims at changing people, including children, towards an end (Quennerstedt & Quennerstedt, 2014). This implies that children's desires and wishes, which affect their choices, decisions and motivation to learn, cannot all of them be afforded and facilitated at school if the school aims are to be achieved. While this is easily understood, this end to which education aims is not defined and determined in consultation with children or even with the majority of adults. This means that participation in decision-making about what takes place in school is limited both for children and for professionals. What serves the best interests of children in school is determined by central governments and is not negotiated with teachers or children. New managerial policies predetermine the areas and their boundaries of issues to be negotiated between teachers and children (*e.g.* Hartley, 1993; Lynch, 2014). The power imbalance between teachers and children is thus exacerbated by the state-imposed, compulsory rules, regulations, curricula and practices. The imposition of ways of working with children makes it difficult for teachers to always offer a child-centered education based on consultation with the children they are responsible for in accordance with the Convention (Osler & Starkey, 1998; Percy-Smith, 2009; Te One & Dalli, 2013).

CHAPTER 2

Models of Schooling and Children's Rights

Abstract: In this chapter, children's rights as defined in the Convention on the rights of the child are related to three models of schooling well known in the Western world. These theoretical models are the traditional, authoritarian school, the school based on traditional developmental psychology and the rights-based school. Aspects of these three models, therefore, may coexist in early years settings in Scotland and Greece and thus facilitate or hinder children from enjoying their rights.

Keywords: Authoritarian school, Convention on the rights of the child, Participation rights, Protection rights, Provision rights, Rights-based school, Traditional-developmental-psychology-based school.

INTRODUCTION

In this chapter, three major conceptualizations of children education are analyzed in order to highlight if and how they afford children their rights as defined by the Convention. The models of schools investigated are the authoritarian, the one based on traditional developmental psychology and the rights-based one. The purpose of such an examination is twofold. First, it sheds light onto solidified school practices, which may hinder the implementation of some of the children's rights. Secondly, aspects of these models of schooling formed part of the empirical research carried out.

The Authoritarian School

In the traditional, authoritarian school, everything that takes place is teacher led (Johnny, 2005). Everything is decided by the adult (Ciccelli, 1983; Mascolo, 2009). The teacher remains in control of the knowledge to be acquired (what is to be learned) by the learners (Wood, 2010) and the learner remains a passive recipient of what the teacher offers and a passive listener, only responding to instructions by the teacher (Johnson & van Wyk, 2016; Kok-Aun, 2014; MacNaughton, 2020; Mascolo, 2009).

Evanthia Synodi
All rights reserved-© 2023 Bentham Science Publishers

Learning in such a school has a theoretical focus, as experience is outcast. It is based on the premise that peers learn in the same way (MacNaughton, 2020), hence the whole class instruction (Kok-Aun, 2014). Learning as acquisition is the metaphor describing education in such a school (Wood, 2010). Therefore, the most common methods of teaching employed are recitation, copying (Ciccelli, 1983; Decker & Decker, 1992, as cited in MacNaughton, 2020; Lowe, 2007), telling, lecturing and direct instruction (Burts, Hart, Charlesworth, Fleege, Mosley, & Thomasson, 1992; Burman, 2008; Johnson & van Wyk, 2016; Kalantzis, Cope, & Harvey 2003; Leininger, 1979; Mascolo, 2009). The curriculum is 'mechanistic – behaviorist' according to Alexander's categorization (1988, as cited in Pugh, 1996, p. 90). There is time and space for the 3 R' s[1] (Lowe, 2007), habit formation, testing and pupil obedience to their teacher and punishment if they do not do as they are told (Ciccelli, 1983; Leininger, 1979; MacNaughton, 2020). This latter aspect of child - teacher relationship is not based on children's rights to physical protection and to the protection of their dignity (articles 19 and 28.2). Space is not abundant in the classroom and time is allocated to activities in a clear cut way (Decker & Decker, 1992, as cited in MacNaughton, 2020; Kok-Aun, 2014; Mascolo, 2009).

In the classroom, the teacher's table is in the front of the rows of desks for pupils and there are sets of textbooks (Kok-Aun, 2014; Walkerdine, 1998). There is no room or time for children to play. Whether children are seen as empty vessels to be filled in schools (Bruce, 1997; Locke, 1689, as cited in Archard, 2004; Kok-Aun, 2014) or as born evil (Archard, 2004; Lowe, 2007) and/or as sinner children (Blenking & Kelly, 1992) and 'in need of redemption' (Lowe, 2007, p. 5), by uprooting this evil from them, 'children need to be schooled to particular ends' (Lowe, 2007, p. 5). Children were considered 'prone to the badness, which only a rigid disciplinary upbringing could correct' (Archard, 2004, p. 46). Parents are supposed to 'break the child's will' (Archard, 2004, p. 46) and their sinfulness and replace it with Christian morality. This duty was extended to schools. A sense of discipline and readiness to accept the rhythms and timing of the working day form part of the aims of the traditional school (Brown, 2014; Hartley, 1993; Lowe, 2007). To achieve these aims, a teacher-led school develops 'subservient conformity, hierarchical acceptance and motivation by external rewards' (Ross, 2008, p. 115, as cited in Brown, 2014, p. 7) in children (MacNaughton, 2020).

In Europe, the mission of a teacher-led school has been moral and sociopolitical (Burman, 2008; Lowe, 2007); to inculcate good habits, and teach 'skills suited to one's gender and station in life' and reading the Bible (Hunt, 1985, as cited in Burman, 2008). The perception of such education for children remains one based on a perception of children as deficient and on the model of passive child (Bruce, 1997; Burman, 2008).

Childhood and thus the education of the children in such a school is a stage of preparation for adulthood. In such a case, respect, protection and implementation of children participation rights, such as their right to be consulted and listened to and to participate in decision making about issues that affect their lives (article 12 UN 1989) are not included. There is provision for the children's right to education (article 28) but not for play (article 31). There is also no protection of human decency and dignity (article 28.2) and of physical safety for the children (article 19). All the above have nothing in common with acknowledging children as rights holders. This approach to children's education is also partly on a par with the protection position (Te One, 2011), which prioritizes children's right to have adults act in their best interest (article 3) but not with the provision thesis (Te One, 2011) because it does not provide for children's right to play (article 31).

The School Based on Traditional Developmental Psychology

The school based on traditional developmental psychology is also governed by a concern for children preparation for adult life (Archard, 2004) as the authoritarian school is. Their difference is in the way of achieving it. Child development is perceived as taking place in stages which determine the level and kind of learning children can achieve (Bruce, 1997; MacNaughton, 2020) and these stages are considered universal (Bruce, 1997; Burman, 2008). Such a school pays attention to the particular features of every stage of the development of the child, rather than train them in the skills they will need as adults (Bruce, 1997). Care and education cannot be compartmentalized and the same applies to learning and development (Hurst, 1991). Holism must characterize adults' perception of children and their education and development (Bruce, 1997).

In this school, there is only the voice of one child who represents each stage of development. Development in areas or in ways other than those discussed by traditional developmental psychology is not accepted as worthwhile (MacNaughton, 2020; Potts, 2007). Falling behind in the development as defined by traditional developmental psychology (Woodhead, 1999) is considered a delay (Bruce, 1997; Curtis, 1998) in unfolding the biological programing of humans, not withstanding cultural and family conditions at least (Potts, 2007; Walkerdine, 1993). Child behavior perceived as diverging from that of the expected stage of development is in need of intervention (Burman, 2008). Family and culture are examined in relation to what can be done to achieve the development corresponding to the learner's age (Popkewitz & Bloch, 2001).

The curriculum in such a school is 'open' and 'negotiable', so as to help children reach their full potential (Alexander, 1988, as cited in Pugh, 1996, p. 90). The activities offered in such a school are either teacher led or child led and a balance between them is recommended, allowing some scope for initiative, action and decision making to children (Bruce, 1997; Ciccelli, 1983; Kok-Aun, 2014). When it comes to learning, children are viewed as scientists who learn and develop when they process their experiences in the company of others (Bruce, 1997). Children individualism and independence must be fostered and choices are offered to them as well as protection from the dangers that supervene the activities children organize (Jans, 2004). The importance of play is acknowledged and prioritized and learning becomes 'hands on', 'tangible' and meaningful to children (David, Curtis, & Siraj-Blatchford, 1993 as cited in Wood & Attfield, 1996, p. 145; see also Bruce, 1997; Curtis, 1998; Hurst, 1991; Kok-Aun, 2014).

In this school, the child is considered a natural, innocent creature in need of protection from adult corruption, which is achieved by separating children from the world of adults (Archard, 2004; Blenkin & Kelly, 1992; Bruce, 1989; Jans, 2004; MacNaughton, 2020; Singer, 1996). However, this school is also based on a belief that the child is 'destructive, asocial and therefore threatening to social order' (Walkerdine & Lucey, 1989, as cited in Burman, 2008, p. 269). Therefore, rules are discussed with children so as to be clarified and to enable children to follow them. The teacher makes the rules concrete and posts them as a chart in the classroom (Warner & Lynch, 2004). This is on a par with the protection position (Te One, 2011) which prioritizes children's right to have adults act in their best interest (article 3) and to be physically protected (article 19). It also agrees with and respects some of the rights prioritized by the proponents of the provision thesis, such as the right to provision for the children's general development (article 29) and for play, spare time and fun (article 31).

This school seems to have some principles and thinking in common with both the provision and the protection theses regarding children's rights. Children are consulted in such a school; however, only when adults see fit in order to assess and plan children learning. In such a school, article 12 is sometimes allowed and respected whereas article 3 takes the form of adults know what is best for the children and have the final word (Singer, 1996). Protecting and providing for the children safety and needs are determined by psychology and applied by teachers. Therefore, what takes place in school (learning, playing, safety *etc.*) is acceptable if it is in congruence with developmental psychology and it is based on 'theories about innate and fixed abilities' (Potts, 2007, p. 65).

The Rights Based School

This is a school where all of the children's rights applicable to school are respected and implemented. The Convention forms part of the content to be taught to children but also affects the practices and life in school (Covell, Howe, &

McNeil, 2010; Osler & Starkey, 1998). Children are allowed not only to learn about their rights, but they and other staff in school respect them and practise them. This means that children are consulted and their views are given attention which respects their age and ability to form an opinion. It also means that children are taught the necessary skills to do so, such as seeking information and expressing themselves in various ways, and are given scope for participating in decision making (Aldreson, 2008; Howe & Covell, 2005; Osler & Starkey, 1998). Such a perception of schooling is based on the model of a child as more capable than traditional psychology has claimed (Woodhead, 1999), a right-holder (Lundy & McEvoy, 2012), and an agent (Kanyal, 2014; Lundy & McEvoy, 2012), even though children do not have all the rights adults have, such as the right to vote for government (*e.g.*Archard, 2004; Jans, 2004).

Regarding children learning, play is important and has influenced the pedagogy suited to a rights-based school. This includes 'games using pictures, role plays, board games, newspaper articles, questionnaires and discussion starters, stories and cartoons' (Osler & Starkey, 1998, p. 317). Teamwork among children is also frequent and considered necessary (Osler & Starkey, 1998).

Rules are discussed with children but not to be clarified so that children follow them. On the contrary, usually at the beginning of the school year, life in the classroom and school as well as rights and responsibilities of all education participants are discussed, negotiated and agreed upon with children. A charter is drawn not excluding anybody in the process which respects children's rights and dignity in accordance with the Convention (Howe & Covell, 2005; Osler & Starkey, 1998).

Therefore, in such a school there is provision for the children's right to education (article 28), to play (article 31), to protection of of their human decency and dignity (article 28.2) and to physical safety (article 19). The establishment of a rights-based school means that articles 3 and 12 are respected as well as children's right to freedom of association and of peaceful assembly in school (article 15) and of children's rights not to be discriminated (article 2).

In the next part of this book, the empirical research undertaken is analyzed in terms of methodology and findings.

NOTES

[1] The 3 R' s are reading, writing and arithmetic (Freeman & Hatch, 1989; Groecke, 1976; Kalantzis, Cope, & Harvey 2003; Leininger, 1979; Morgan & Robinson, 1976; Ross, 1980).

EMPIRICAL RESEARCH PART

This part of the study is dedicated to describing the methodology of conducting this empirical research and the data from the focus group sessions with children aged 5 to 6 years from Scotland and Greece. In the methodology chapter, it is explained that this is a comparative research with a qualitative approach to producing data. Focus groups sessions with five year old children were conducted. The reasons for selecting the specific countries and children are explained as well as the process of the research. At the end of the chapter, the ethical considerations of the research and the measures taken to ensure its trustworthiness are analyzed.

The methodology chapter is followed by four chapters of data analysis; three chapters devoted to the first focus group sessions and one chapter devoted to the second sessions. During the first sessions, children discussed three types of schools; a traditional, authoritarian school, a school based on traditional developmental psychology and a rights-based school in terms of their physical environment and social environment. In our second sessions, the children were read a part of the book called *Whiffy Wilson, the wolf who wouldn't go to school* and then made suggestions as to what school would make Wilson want to attend it.

CHAPTER 3

Methodology

Abstract: This chapter is dedicated to the empirical research undertaken in order to discover, first, children's perceptions on aspects of provision and practices, pre-selected by me, which have characterized theories and policies about classes for five to six year old children. A second purpose of carrying out this study is to discover what aspects of a school for children of their age these children consider essential. All data is discussed in terms of respect or violation of children's rights in order to highlight the connection of children's views with children's rights. It is a comparative research conducted in a qualitative manner using focus groups. The sample is five to six year old children who attended school in Scotland and Greece and participated in two focus group sessions. Approval for this research with children was granted by the appropriate authorities both in Scotland and Greece. Permission to conduct the research with children was requested by their teachers, their parents, and the children themselves. Finally, the measures taken to ensure that this research research is conducted in accordance with research ethics and issues on its trustworthiness are discussed.

Keywords: Comparative education, Early childhood education, Focus groups, Primary school, Qualitative research, Research trustworthiness, Rights based school, Research ethics, School based on traditional developmental psychology, Teacher-directed school.

INTRODUCTION

The reason for this study, for its purpose and its design, is based on my working as an educator and not a child sociologist. As such a person, I have seen, observed and spoken to teachers, both in Greece and some parts of Europe, of young children about working with them. Their ways of working and being with children seemed to me that sometimes did not indicate acknowledgement of children as right holders. At times, some teachers' behavior did not show any awareness of them violating some of the children's rights or even that children had rights at school. Whether they believed they should treat children like that or were forced to is beyond the aims of this study. However, I wanted to find out how children felt about the different school practices and provisions, which respected or violated some of their rights.

Evanthia Synodi
All rights reserved-© 2023 Bentham Science Publishers

Therefore, this study is dedicated to children in Scotland and Greece expressing their views on aspects of school practice in schools for children aged five to six years. I did not intend to conduct emancipatory research (Cohen, Manion, & Morrison, 2018) or share the topic and design of the research with children (Thomas, 2021). I only wanted to give children a chance to express how they felt about specific behaviors and practices which take place or are likely to take place in classes for five years olds, so that I can relate these ideas to children's rights.

More specifically, the purpose of this study is to explore five-year-old children's views on aspects of behavior and rules, learning and play and the physical environment in schools so that I can relate these views to their rights. The aspects of school practice and school provision selected for this study reflect the implementation or not of various provision, protection and participation rights that children are entitled to in schools. Therefore, this research aims to examine (a) how children feel about specific (selected by me) aspects of school practice and provision for five to six year old children, and (b) what specific aspects of an education for children of their age children themselves consider important in order to determine what children's rights these views reflect.

Background to the Conceptualization of this Research

Two pieces of research related to young children's perceptions of school guided me in selecting the particular aspects of schooling to be studied. They are a research by Sheridan and Pramling-Samuelsson (2001) and a research by Einarsdottir (2005).

According to Sheridan and Pramling-Samuelsson (2001), when young children in Sweden were asked to define what it means to decide, the children referred to (a) what they want to do, mostly during play and free activity time, (b) what is allowed and what is not and (c) the exercise of power and control. Children seemed to categorize decisions at school into decisions made by teachers, decisions made by groups of children and decisions made by each child individually. As for who decides what happens at school, children claimed that the teacher decides about almost everything, such as the conditions in the school, everyday routines, rules, norms and values as well as handling little daily incidents. According to almost all of the participating children, they do not decide where and when they play. Many times they felt that their teachers' decisions had priority over what they wanted to do. Children believed that the only decisions allowed to them were relevant to what they would play, what their own free activities would be and what to do with their belongings. Children also said that they co-decided things with their teachers only when they are going to do an activity together, such as a circle time activity. As a group of peers, children decided, all together, what to do and mainly what to play but children knew that some of them decided more often than others.

Einarsdottir (2005) found that children in Iceland considered that the teacher's role included disciplining and controlling children on top of teaching. Teachers handled children's disputes and ensured that children followed the rules. Children also said that they did not like participating in group activities over which they did not have any control and during which they had to follow their teachers' instructions. When asked what they could decide and what not, children in Iceland, in the same way as children in Sweden, said that they were allowed to decide about their play and their free activities. At the same time, however, they understood that their choices of play and games were not unlimited and that they would need to wait at times because of the large number of children waiting in a queue to play in a specific area. Children also mentioned that they could not decide about the general operation of the school, the routine, the rules, their diet as well as the activities and their content, which were organised by adults, just like in Sweden. The list of the issues children felt they were not allowed to decide is as follows:

What classroom we are in

When we go outdoors

When we play with the computer

What the playschool teachers do

What we have for lunch

What we draw in philosophy-time

Where you sit

When to leave choice time

When to leave rest time

Where to be at rest time

To ruin things if the playschool teacher leaves

To sneak out

To climb over the fence

To sneak away and go home

To run in the hallway

To sleep

To hurt other people

To change the rules

To be rude (Einarsdottir, 2005, p. 482).

Both studies aimed at linking children's views with the quality of the preschool provision they received. However, their data also suggest that article 12 needs more scope for implementation in the schools under examination. Children expressed aspects of decision-making that they wanted to be consulted about but adults would not or were not allowed to let them.

Some of the aspects of provision and practice for five-year-olds that children in these two studies referred to were selected for this research and grouped into two categories; the physical environment of the school and the social environment of the school. Play and learning, in terms of time, space and resources formed part of the physical environment, whereas teachers' and children's tasks and duties at school in terms of acceptable behavior, relationships and rules formed part of the social environment of a school in this study.

Comparative Study

Children's views on the above educational events, *i.e.* aspects of schooling, were produced in two countries, because of the significance I attribute to conducting a comparative study in education. The significance of comparison lies in leading the researcher into a deeper understanding of the education phenomena and events they study and the impact of societal factors (*e.g.* economy, governance, politics, culture) on the education phenomena under study (Calogiannaki, 2011; Clarkson, 2009; Georgeson, Payler, & Cambell-Barr, 2013; Kazamias, 2009; Khoi, 1981, as cited in Bouzakis, 1993; Lubeck, 1995; Phillips & Schweisfurth, 2011). I consider this very important because it allows us to determine if there are common answers to these events and to what extent in these two countries and to reflect on the possible reasons for this to happen. To achieve the purpose of a Comparative Education study there must be careful consideration of the selection of countries so that they are not too different (Clarkson, 2009). The education for five-year-old children in Scotland and Greece was selected for various reasons so as to enable the study to be viable, productive, worthwhile and manageable (Clarkson, 2009).

Scotland and Greece were chosen because of their difference in economic affluence and what it entails for their education systems. Scotland, as part of the United Kingdom [UK][1], was selected because it is considered a rich country, whereas Greece is struggling to survive. Less developed capitalists countries, like Greece, have education systems which waste their human capital (Filias, 1989), whereas metropolitan capitalist countries, like the United Kingdom (part of which is Scotland), exhaust all their resources, including their human capital (Gizeli, 1987; Socolova, Kouzmina, & Rodionof, 1990). These differences in affluence mean that there is less financial aid to education in Greece as compared to Scotland. The economic differences may push teachers to prioritize their school needs on their own and in accordance with legislation. In such a case, financial constraints have the potential to minimize the opportunities for children to assert their rights and for their contributions on school provision to be requested and considered.

Another reason for selecting these two countries were three particular differences in their national cultures with culture defined as 'the collective programming of the mind distinguishing the members of one group or category of people from others' (Hofstede, 2021a) or as 'the set of norms, behaviors, beliefs, customs, and values shared by the population of a sovereign nation' (Berrell, 2020). It 'also refers to specific characteristics such as language, religion, ethnic and racial identity, and cultural history and traditions' (Berrell, 2020). I, influenced by comparativists such as Kandel (1933, as cited in Calogiannaki, 2011; Kazamias, 2009; Potts, 2007), accept that national cultures can affect both how things are done in education and children's experiences in general and, thus, children's views about their education. However, the dimensions of each national culture I selected are not going to be used in an essentialist way, that is as determinants of the children's views. I intend to examine if they can be linked to the views expressed within and across the countries, because my understanding is that national cultures are influenced both by the existence of a dominant culture[2] as well as the existence of other co-cultures[3] in any country.

The three cultural dimensions between Greece and the United Kingdom as defined and measured by Hofstede that I find relevant to the topic of children's education and their rights are power distance (Hofstede, 2019a), indulgence (Hofstede, 2019b) and individualism (Hofstede, 2021b). The dimension of power distance.

'Expresses the degree to which the less powerful members of a society [4] accept and expect that power is distributed unequally. The fundamental issue here is how a society handles inequalities among people' (Hofstede, 2019a).

The score on power distance is higher for Greece (Hofstede, 2019a); it is almost double compared with that of the UK (60 versus 35). This may manifest in the form of children expecting or even receiving more adult directed education from their teachers in Greece and thus children's scope for consultation or participation in a Greek school may be narrower.

Indulgence is defined as

'The extent to which people try to control their desires and impulses, based on the way they were raised'. ... 'People in societies classified by a high score in indulgence generally exhibit a willingness to realize their impulses and desires with regard to enjoying life and having fun' (Hofstede, 2019b).

In terms of indulgence, the UK scores a lot higher (Hofstede, 2019b) than Greece (69 versus 50). The higher the score, the more likely it is that children in Scotland want to satisfy their desires and not to be constrained. However, the same goes for their teachers who may not want any constraints posed by children on what teachers plan for them. This clash can cause a power struggle between children's right to be consulted and express their views and teachers deciding on their own what is in the best interest of the children under their care.

As far as individualism is concerned, Greece scores only 35 as compared to 91 for UK. This means that people in Scotland are:

'Private people. Children are taught from an early age to think for themselves and to find out what their unique purpose in life is and how they uniquely can contribute to society' (Hofstede, 2021b).

As Farlane (2018, p. 133) explains in the Anglosphere (part of which is Scotland) schools teach children 'to be independent, to think and act for' themselves, 'to make' their 'own decisions, to distance' themselves, 'to exercise self-control'. On the other hand, in Greece children become members of strong groups that protect them and to whom children owe loyalty (Hofstede, 2021b; see also Farlane, 2018). This difference, too, may have some impact on children's views on their education, as it is more likely that children in Greece are taught to depend on or allow adults to decide for them a lot more than in Scotland.

Within any country, school cultures, dominant or not, are:

'The historically transmitted patterns of meaning that include the norms, values, beliefs, ceremonies, rituals, traditions, and myths understood, maybe in varying degrees, by members of the school community' and affect 'what people think and how they act' (Stolp & Smith, 1994, as cited in Stolp, 1994, p. 2).

Furthermore, there is also each person's culture, that is, 'how we relate to other people, how we think, how we behave and how we view the world' (Rodriguez, 1999, as cited in Samovar, Porter, McDaniel, & Roy, 2013, p. 35). This is a definition of culture that shows how individuals, including teachers and children, do not learn or accept all the elements of the culture in which they are brought up and / or live in (Keesing, 1974), that is, of the culture as the 'group worldview, the way of organizing the world that a particular society has created over time' (Nolan, 1999, as cited in Samovar *et al.*, 2013, p. 35).

The above show that teachers' cultures may vary and not be on a par with some school policies or some school cultures (see also Warren Little, 1993). Teachers may also have different cultures in the sense that they may not agree with the dominant culture (Samovar *et al.*, 2013) whether that is located in the country where they work or in their school. Moreover, they have different education and training backgrounds, which contribute to teachers' cultures and thus to their various degrees of identification with the education policy, central or devolved, which they have to implement. This means that they may interpret children's rights and any top down policies they have to implement in different ways or disagree with some of their aspects, if not the whole of them (see also Jones & Welch, 2018; Scott, 2008; Troman, 1996). As Bowe, Ball, and Gold (1992, p. 22) claim 'practitioners do not confront policy texts as passive readers and policy writers cannot control the meaning of their texts'. Teachers' cultures, therefore, may vary and influence their commitment to implementing children's rights beyond any directions from above about how teachers should work.

Additionally, in countries where curricula are centrally imposed and highly perscriptive, these together with other optional and non-optional policy documents influence, reform and change school cultures and subsequently teachers' cultures to varying degrees. This is likely to happen across and within Scotland and Greece because, as I have already explained, I accept that people identify to different degrees with their national culture and other co-cultures they are in contact with. Furthermore, Hofstede discusses frequencies and percentages of the dimensions found in each culture and, so, one cannot know which schools and their cultures are representative of the most frequent dimension or not.

Therefore, depending on the culture of the school children attend and their teacher's culture, children may have different perceptions of the best school provision for them based on different priorities. At the same time children's background and cultures, regardless of whether they are taken into account or not, may vary, just like their teachers'. What I mean is that there is cultural diversity in the countries in Europe, part of which is Scotland and Greece, regardless of whether they are perceived as homogeneous or multi-ethnic societies, because of the history of nation-building in Europe (*e.g.* Aman, 2018; Green, 1990), because of the varying degrees of people's independence to think and live in various ways in Europe as well as because of the variety of cultures in the world. This diversity means that children in school in these two countries may not hold the same perceptions of what their education should be like.

Another basic difference between the education systems of Scotland and Greece is very important for the richness of data this comparison can yield. Five-year-old children in Scotland attend primary school for the first time, whereas their peers in Greece attend kindergartens. Primary education begins at 6 years in Greece and exhibits a distinct change in the character of teaching, which becomes academically orientated, and in the time allocated to play, which is diminished. This basic difference in the official education for five-year-olds in these two countries then is translated into more time for play allowed to children in Greece because they go to kindergarten as compared to children in Scotland who go to primary school. However, Scotland has at least two decades of child-centered primary education starting in 1965 (Darling 2004) more than Greece. Child-centeredness as a means of facilitating the respect and implementation of young children's rights (General Comment 7, 2005, articles 14, 17, 23, 28, and 34), therefore, exists in some form or another in the official educational provision in both countries.

Simultaneously, Greece and Scotland have similarities that justify their selection for comparison. They are both located in Europe, were both parts of the European Union when the empirical research in Scotland took place and are countries with mainly a Christian population and past (U.S Department of State, Report on International Religious Freedom: Greece, 2017; U.S Department of State, Report on International Religious Freedom: United Kingdom, 2017), even though this tendency is stronger in Greece (98% compared to 54% in Scotland). Therefore, over the centuries, people in Scotland and Greece have known aspects of similar cultures, philosophies, and ideas, whether in terms of national cultures or of co-cultures in each country in a way that countries, for example, in America or Africa as former colonies have known[5] more recently. This means that not all children within the same country or between two countries have the same culture, needs or priorities, however defined, and thus there is not one version of children's voice in each country. In this study, the term voice is used as Jones and Welch (2018) define it rather than as related to children's agency and participation determined by childhood studies (Lee, 1998). I employed the term voice because many children are still 'silenced, not listened to or have adults speak for them' most of the times decisions are made for them and without any other connotations (Jones & Welch, 2018, p. 118).

The above mean that these two countries, which have some cultural (in terms of white, European culture) and religious similarities which can help comparison[6], also have economic and societal - cultural differences in between them which enable the researcher to understand the education phenomena (Calogiannaki, 2015) under study more deeply.

The final reason for choosing Scotland and Greece is a practical one. I refer to having chosen to use an oral method of investigation, focus group, which I analyze further later in this chapter. Since children in Greece are not officially taught to read and write at 5 years and I am a native Greek speaker and a fluent speaker of English I chose a Greek-speaking and an English-speaking country. This also enabled me to ensure linguistic equivalence, which should characterize every comparative study (Broadfoot, Osborn, with Gilly, & Bûcher, 1993).

The data for this comparison was chosen to be produced qualitatively.

Qualitative Research

This study gave children the opportunity to express their views on some school matters affecting them, *i.e.* behaviour and routine, rules, teacher-organized activities, play and the physical environment. Therefore, this is research about some children's voices and not the voice of children in general or their full participation in the design, implementation and analysis of this research (Elden, 2012). However, I have borrowed many elements of organizing and conducting a research that are advocated by childhood studies when designing the research. This is a qualitative study in which the control of the research lies with the adult researcher and, as already explained, the term voice is employed because there is a tendency to silence young children, in particular, not to listen to them or have adults speak for them (Jones & Welsh, 2018) regardless of whether they are mature enough and capable of forming a view (article 12). I have recorded voices of five to six year old boys and girls from Scotland and Greece who were nationals in each country, native speakers of the official language of their countries, able-bodied and did not have learning difficulties.

Since I was not the participants' teacher, I could not have taken action in terms of (a) What happens in their schools and of (b) Providing for space, voice, audience and influence in their schools (Lundy, 2007). I can only hold an 'enlightenment position', as Warshak (2003, pp. 373-374) calls it, and influence in different ways on the topics I have selected to investigate. As a teacher educator, I can inform my students about children's preferences and opinions so that, based on them, they can provide for children's rights and learn that they are required to consult with their pupils. I can also inform in-service teachers so that they can discuss issues with their pupils or continue their effective and respectful to children's rights practice.

To achieve the aim of producing and recording children's perceptions on aspects of practice and provision in school, a qualitative approach to research was considered appropriate. The purpose of a qualitative approach to research is to investigate the lives of people, their experiences, attitudes, behaviors and feelings (Straus & Corbin, 1998). This approach is based on the rationale that people, such as the children in this study, actively construct their meanings and use these interpretations of theirs to act (Cohen, Manion, & Morrison, 2018). These meanings and interpretations are multiple, 'context-bound' and 'culture-bound' (Cohen, Manion, & Morrison, 2018, p. 288). A qualitative methodology helps to understand how the world or a part of it, such as a school, operates in the opinion of its participants because it studies their perspectives and their experiences (Cohen, Manion, & Morrison, 2018; Gotowos, 1983; Hatch, 1995).

This study is exploratory since there is a limited number of such studies, particularly in Greece, and because of its comparative character. The qualitative approach is realized by employing focus groups, a method that does not aim to affirm or dismiss hypotheses but to produce data about a topic (Flick, 2007).

Method

To investigate this broad topic, focus groups (Flick, 2007; Large & Beheshti, 2001) were selected as a method of producing data. With this method, the researcher organises a small group of children who discuss a topic and their experiences of it (Gibson, 2007; Kitzinger, 1994). The role of the researcher is that of a facilitator, helping children express their thoughts and influence each other so as to form views and attitudes regarding the topic by themselves (Kitzinger, 1995; Robinson, 1999; Wilson, 1997). Focus groups do not imply that children have already formed views and attitudes about what they are going to discuss, the same way an interview does for example (Kitzinger, 1995). They allow children to think about things, exchange arguments with other children and form an opinion because of their specific discussions in groups. Discussions in focus groups are child-led and do not look like a classroom dialogue where the adult asks questions and the children answer. Furthermore, focus groups were selected because the role of the researcher is not all pervasive and gives children the opportunity to express themselves (Gibson, 2007). This way the power imbalance between the researcher and participants can be reduced in favour of the children.

The sessions were accompanied by the non-verbal expression of children's thoughts and views through drawing. Works such as that of Colucci (2007) influenced the methodology of the focus group sessions in this study. Colucci (2007) reports a number of activities that should accompany focus group sessions with children, either before, during or after the sessions (see also Kitzinger, 1994; Robinson, 1999). Such activities can be free listings, rating scales, rankings, pile sorting, choosing the best alternative, labelling, magic tools and fantasy, stories, role-playing, collage, filling in the gaps, and painting (Colucci, 2007, pp. 1424-1429). Following her advice, I wrote stories for the first session and used part of a storybook for the second session (see also Gibson, 2007) and asked children to draw their ideas about what they discussed in their group after each session.

Research Tools

As already mentioned, I used focus groups to generate data and I had two sessions with each group of children. In the first focus group session, children were asked to discuss three different stories, which regarded topics in three different models of school - the traditional / authoritarian, the one based on developmental psychology and the rights-based one. In the second session, to elicit children's views on the desired education for five year olds, children were given the opportunity to describe and discuss whatever they thought was necessary for the best school ever after listening to the beginning of the story *Whiffy Wilson: the wolf who wouldn't go to school* (Hart, 2014).

The First Focus Group Session

For the first session, I wrote stories for the participating children to discuss. I chose to write stories about the problem of planning the best school for five to six year old children, which children were asked to discuss. Children like stories and I wanted to have something concrete, so to speak, for them to discuss and for me to refer to when asking my questions. The stories were written in a respectful manner showing my genuine belief that children could answer me and to show this appreciation of their input I wrote about a queen and a king, powerful adults, asking for their advice, solutions and suggestions.

Therefore, the topics described in the stories involved two broad aspects of the school environment: the physical and the social. In terms of the physical environment, the onus was on variations in resources and spaces for play and child-initiated activities and, implicitly, in time for play and child-initiated activities. The more resources for play the larger the spaces in the school. Time was only implied in the description of what the teacher allows children to do as children and not as her pupils. So, the environments varied from few resources, small spaces (not allowing for much movement and gross mobility) and little time to play, to a variety of resources, larger spaces and more time for child-initiated activities to a greater selection of resources, spacious schools and children determining their schedule (I was influenced by school practices in Summerhill).

In terms of social environment, behaviors towards one's teacher and one's peers ranged from appropriate behavior almost entirely determined by the teacher (I believe that not all aspects of behavior and action can be controlled) to children being allowed to partly determine some behaviors as appropriate to appropriate behavior being determined by both teacher and children.

These stories included the aspects of education I selected from the research by Sheridan and Pramling-Samuelsson (2001) and by Einarsdottir (2005). They were also adjusted to reflect the three conceptualizations of school with whatever they entail in terms of implementing children's rights and the varying degrees of power imbalance between adults and children, which these conceptualizations entail. These ranged from children having some freedom only during breaks (*e.g.* what to do / play), to children having some individual choices allowed by adults (*e.g.* selecting from the offered by the teacher free activities) to children being allowed to co-decide about their education (*e.g.* being allowed artifacts and content relevant to their societal cultures) with their teachers. In terms of culture, I want to remind you that I wrote stories about schools in Europe and asked children from Europe, so, I refer to education theories that have informed ideas about young children and education philosophy and policy in Europe.

Plans for Schools for Young Children

The stories about the physical and social environment of the schools were based on my interpretation of basic characteristics related by educators known in Europe to three different conceptualizations of education and schools, analyzed in Chapter 2. These are:

1. The traditional school, based on behaviorism and influenced by the models of the child as a sinner and as an empty vessel (Bruce, 1997).

2. The school based on traditional developmental psychology (also known as child-centered) and on the models of the child as innocent and as a scientist (Bruce, 1997).

3. The rights-based school, influenced by the sociology of childhood and childhood studies and the models of the child as competent and as a right holder.

The rights which can be related to education in school are many but not all of them were selected for this study. The rights pertaining to school and were not included in the study were children's rights not to be discriminated due to their different culture (article 31), religion (articles 14 and 30) and language (articles 29(d)- 30) while in school. There was also no reference made to children's rights to have their different needs provided for (article 23), to be protected from substance and sexual abuse (articles 33-34) and from economic or other types of exploitation (articles 32 and 36) while in school. Children's right not to be discriminated (article 2) was included only in the rights-based model of school. The reason for the exclusion of these rights was twofold. Firstly, there was no direct reference to them in the two guiding published research works by Sheridan and Pramling Samuelsson (2001) and Einarsdottir (2005). Secondly, because the stories would become too large and full of details for their young audience. The rest of the children rights which are applicable to the three models of school and relevant to the selected items from the above two researches are analyzed in the description of each story about it.

The Authoritarian School

Based on the philosophy of an authoritarian school and on features from the studies by Sheridan and Pramling-Samuelsson (2001) and by Einarsdottir (2005), the plan for a teacher-centered school is as follows:

'Once upon a time there lived a queen and a king in a land of forests. They decided to build schools for young children in their country. Their helpers made a plan for a school and gave it to the queen and the king.

In this school, the teacher will make all the decisions for the children. She will set the classroom rules for the children without asking them and she will punish them when they do not follow them. The teacher will prepare lessons for the children and all of them will do the same thing at the same time. All the children will sit quietly and listen to their teacher. When there is a break, the teacher will let the children play for a while. Then she will stop them and start her lesson again.

Around the school, there will be high wire netting. The yard will be small, covered in cement and have a few trees. Inside the school there will be rows of desks, a blackboard, a clock on the wall and a large desk for the teacher.

The queen and king read this plan carefully and then decided to invite young children to talk about this school and tell them how they feel about it. Can we help them plan the best school ever?'

The Developmental Psychology based School

The plan for a school based on developmental psychology and the elements of the studies by Sheridan and Pramling-Samuelsson (2001) and by Einarsdottir (2005) is the as follows:

'Once upon a time there lived a queen and a king in a land of forests. They decided to build schools for young children in their country. Their helpers made a plan for a school and gave it to the queen and king.

In this school, the teacher and the children will decide together about many issues but not about everything. The teacher will set some rules but she will also make some with the children. The teacher will prepare activities which she thinks children like. She will sometimes play with them in the corners and in the yard as if she were a little child herself. She will let children play a lot but she will want lessons, too.

Around the school building there will be a hedge. The yard will be large and some of it will be covered with grass and some of it with tartan. The yard will also have trees, a sand pit, a play house, a climber and a slide. Inside the school, there will be large rooms and a lot of stuff for the children such as toys, books, dolls, crayons, small tables and chairs and a clock. There will be no rows of desks or a big desk for the teacher.

The queen and king read this plan carefully and then decided to invite young children to talk about this school and tell them how they feel about it. Can we help them plan the best school ever?'

The Rights based School

In the plan I wrote for a rights-based school I did not include certain rights, which, nevertheless, should be respected in a rights-based school. The rights that were not included in this study were children's right to their enjoying their cultures (article 31), religions (articles 14 and 30) and mother tongues (articles 29(d) - 30) while in school, to having their different needs catered for (article 23), to protection from substance and sexual abuse (articles 33-34), from economic or other types of exploitation (articles 32 and 36) and from discimination (article 2). However, in the plan for a right-based school, the only criterion of discrimination included was children not being discriminated due to their young age alone.

Discrimination due to youth would come under the violation of article 12 of the Convention which includes age as well as capacity to form opinions as a criterion of considering children's views when decisions are being made on issues affecting them. Therefore, the plan for the rights-based school is as follows:

'Once upon a time there lived a queen and a king in a land of forests. The queen and a king decided to build schools for young children in their country. The queen and king invited all the children to the palace. The children could come alone or with their friends or with their family. All of them together, grown-ups and children, decided what their school would look like and what they will do in the school.

In this school, the children and the teachers will decide together about all the school problems. They will decide (a) what they will do with children and teachers who do not treat others well or (b) if they go visit a museum. In this school the children and the teachers will decide all of the rules together. The teacher will ask the children what they want to do and learn and that is what they will do.

Children will play everywhere in the school; in the corners, in the gym, in the yard and in the forest with their teachers and with other children. Their teachers will never interrupt their play to start other activities. They will not put wire or bushes around the yard. The school yard will have grass but also tartan. There will also be trees, a sand pit, a play house, a jungle gym, a seesaw, a climber and a slide. The school will have large and tiny rooms. They will put a lot of stuff inside for the children, such as toys, books, teddy bears, crayons, tricycles, dough, furniture, big and small, cement, plaster, wood, thermometers, tubes, scissors, spatulas, knives and saws.

The queen and king read this plan carefully and then decided to invite other young children to talk about this school and tell them how they feel about it. Can we help them plan the best school ever?'

I read these stories to the children of different groups of five year olds in Scotland and Greece. The main questions asked were: What should we keep from this plan so as to make the best school ever? and What should we change? As a facilitator, I was prepared to ask children to discuss the social environment of the schools, in terms of rules and appropriate behavior, and the physical environment, in terms of resources and what they mean for space and time in school.

After this discussion, children were invited to draw one thing they could decide in their school and one thing that they wanted to do in school but they were not allowed to. This was a way I selected to deal with the possibility that children would not discuss or answer questions about education outside the plan.

Second Focus Group Session

In a second session, the groups were read the first part of the story *Whiffy Wilson: The wolf who wouldn't go to school* (Hart, 2014). Even though Wilson has never been to school, he thought school was boring, learning to read and write useless and teachers get angry when children make mistakes. He would rather stay home and sleep or watch television. This was the part of the book I read to children:

'There was a wolf called Wilson who couldn't count to ten. He wouldn't learn to write his name. He never used a pen. He didn't know his A B Cs. He couldn't paint or cook. He wouldn't learn his two-plus-twos. He never read a book.

'Time for school!' his father cried, 'you pesky little pup!'.

'But school is BORING!' Wilson whined, and he turned the telly up.

One morning, Wilson went next door to ask his friend to play. But Dotty smiled, 'I can't because I'm off to school today.'

'Well, I'm not going', Wilson grumped. 'Who wants to read and write? I'd rather play and watch TV and stay up late at night.'

'Oh, you're so silly', Dotty smiled. 'Come to school with me! There's nothing to be scared of - school's lots of fun, you'll see!'

'WHO SAYS I'M SCARED?' growled Wilson. 'A wolf is brave and strong. It's just ... the teacher might be cross if I get the answers wrong.'

I stopped reading the story at this point and I asked children *'What school would make Wilson want to attend it?'* So, instead of listening to Wilson's friend's reasons for attending school (the part which I did not read to the children), children were asked to describe the type of school that would make Wilson want to go to school. When children gave all their suggestions, they were asked to draw this school. By doing this, each child was allowed to express what was important to them in a school Whiffy would like to attend after hearing their classmates' ideas, too. This way I attempted to collect the priorities of each focus group on the best school for a young child.

Research Questions

As already stated, the purpose of this study is to explore the views of five year old children in Greece and Scotland on specific aspects of the physical and the social environment of a school. Therefore, the design of the first session aimed to answer the following questions:

1. Which aspects of the school plans presented to them are children in favor of? Which rights do these aspects refer to?

2. Which aspects of the school plans presented to them are children not in favor of? Which rights do these aspects refer to?

The second focus group session allowed children more freedom in describing their views on a school for young children, as it was initiated by reading them only the beginning of the story of Wilson. According to the story, Wilson did not want to go to school, so, children were asked to discuss what school may make him want to attend. Through this session I attempted to answer the following question:

3. Which particular aspects of school provision and practices do children prioritize and include when imagining the best school for Wilson and by default for young children? Which rights do the children's views reflect?

The answers to this question show which rights are important to them and which rights these children are not yet ready to handle or even perceive they have.

The comparative nature of this research poses an extra dimension to all the research questions:

4. Are children's views similar or different across countries? On which aspects of schooling? For what possible reason?

5. Are children's views similar or different within each country? On which aspects of schooling? For what possible reason?

Sample and Participants

The sample of the children who participated in this study is a sample of convenience (Robson, 2007; Verma & Mallick, 2004) but it also snowballed (Cohen, Manion, & Morrison, 2018). It comprises five groups of children from three Primary 1 classes from two schools in Scotland and nine groups of children from eight classes in three schools in Greece. The intention was to work with nine to twelve children aged 5 to 6 from each country. Despite being a convenience sample, a lot more children were allowed to participate by headteachers, teachers and parents and were willing to help me themselves, so my sampling snowballed. In the end, 20 children in Scotland and 36 from Greece participated.

The sessions took place in Scotland in the third school term of 2016 and in Greece in the third school term of 2017. The third school term was selected so that children had time to experience their new class and school. Each session lasted between 45-60 minutes; up to 30 minutes were spent on me reading to them the plans or the story and on their discussion by the children and up to 30 minutes for drawing.

Research Ethics

Official Permission for Research

Permissions to conduct research in schools were granted by the University of Edinburgh in Scotland (February 2016) and the Ministerial Department of Education in Greece (June 2016). The schools were selected based on their cooperation with teaching staff in Moray House School of Education, University of Edinburgh and with the Department of Preschool Education, University of Crete and on their willingness to accept me to conduct research with their children.

Contact with Research Gatekeepers

When the permission was granted, I prepared information sheets for the headteachers. Once they accepted to allow me into their school, I gave them information sheets and consent forms for the parents of their five-year-old pupils (Flewitt, 2005). These were distributed to parents by the school teachers. When I had the parental permissions, the teachers of these children decided who would be a member of each of the groups. My only request to teachers was that they form groups of children who get along so that they do not fight with each other during the sessions.

Anonymity

The schools were given pseudonyms to protect the children's anonymity. The two school from Scotland whose children participated in the research were named Valley School and Hill School and the three schools from Greece were named Elm School, Oak School and Pine School.

The groups of children who took part in the study were further named as it was required for the second focus group session. In Scotland, the two groups from Hill School who were read the plans for a teacher centered school and developmental psychology based school participated with the same composition in the second session. In Greece, only children from Oak School participated in the same group in both sessions.

On the other hand, children from Valley School and one group from Hill School in Scotland and children from Elm School and Pine School in Greece participated in different groups in the second session. That was so because some children were absent when I visited their school for the session of their group. These absences of children in either the first or the second focus group session led to some groups being comprised of five children instead of four, as initially planned and to the need for a new name for their groups. These were MX, AU, DP And RB. MX stands for mixed group and it means that its children had discussed different plans in their first session with me. The groups of children who were read the plan for an authoritarian, school were named AU, the groups who were read the plan for a developmental psychology based school were named DP and the groups who were read the plan for a rights-based school were named RB.

Research Process

I spoke with each group of children at the beginning of our first session. I asked the children if they wanted to help a queen and a king find out what the best school for children is like according to the children themselves. When they replied possitively (which was always the case), I explained that they were not obliged to participate and that they could leave at any moment they felt uncomfortable. They were informed that the identity of whoever spoke and about whomever they spoke as well as whatever they tell me would be *our secret*. To ensure their anonymity in the public presentation of their views, whenever necessary, children were given pseudonyms. Finally, I explained to them that I would use a recording device to record our talk because I could not remember everything, yet I wanted to keep everything they told me because it was valuable. These details were also given to children in the form of information sheets, which they kept and I also gave them assent forms to sign (Flewitt, 2005). None of the children refused to help me or withdrew from the study. However, there were very few children, mainly in the sample from Scotland, that were absent from school the day one of their two sessions was scheduled.

Power Issues

To minimize the power imbalance between the researcher and children, prior to our sessions I spent time with them as a child, as Nancy Mandell did (1991). This was done so that we could build rapport and some degree of trust. By spending time with them, as if I were a child as much as it is possible, I also wanted to show children that I respected them and perceived them as people whose company and ideas I appreciated. I played with the children in both countries during breaks if they asked me, yet children in Scotland always asked me to play with them when they were not being taught.

Furthermore, teachers in Scotland asked me if I could help teams of children with their work in class[7]. I saw this as a positive opportunity to build a relationship with the children, regardless of whether they would be my participants or not, by helping them. It was an opportunity for me to become a part of the classroom daily routine, someone who assisted children with whatever they did not remember or understand of their teacher's lesson. I tried to perceive myself and act as a child's assistant rather than a classroom assistant; as somebody who was there to relieve children of stress caused by their miscomprehensions or disinterestedness in lessons and tasks (Gibson, 2007).

Ensuring the Trustworthiness of the Research

To ensure the trustworthiness of a research, one must provide for the credibility, dependability, transferability and confirmability (Lincoln & Guba, 1985) of the study. In terms of research design and research approach and methodology, my prolonged engagement with children and teachers in schools was helpful not only in terms of research ethics (discussed earlier) but also in terms of credibility (Lincoln & Guba, 1985) and of accuracy and reliability of the data compared (Clarkson, 2009). The advantages of prolonged engagement were also accomplished by me spending time in an early years center serving children aged one up to nearly six, in one nursery school and one nursery class before embarking into the empirical research in Scotland. Especially the visits to the early years center worked as a pilot in many ways, as the headteacher, her staff and the parents of the children attending allowed me to organize activities, both learning and research ones, with the children. I had the opportunity to learn and understand the terminology and practices used in schools and the context in which they operated. This was also necessary because I had been working within the Greek education system and had never been in any school or educare institution in Scotland before. This way I also ensured observational flexibility and credible equivalence to provide for the trustworthiness of the comparative research and against the researcher's bias (Clarkson, 2009; Kay-Flowers, 2009).

As for credibility during the focus group sessions, one rule I followed was to prepare probing questions in advance and be prepared to ask probing and clarification questions to stimulate the discussions, because not all children have the same level of language development at the same age. I tried not to use complex words or syntax structures. I also tried to summarize what the children told me so that they confirm that I understood them correctly because they may have not understood my language as an adult but also because I may not have understood theirs as children, especially if it was not Greek. Another rule I followed was to not push the discussions during the focus group sessions especially with 'feeling and experience' questions that may have been raised (Patton, 1980, as cited in Cohen, Manion, & Morrison, 2018, p. 515).

Transferability in the form of reader's generalizability is very important to this study (Noble & Smith, 2015; Shenton, 2004) in the sense that other educators are able to identify thoughts and behaviors of their pupils with thoughts and behaviors of the participants and profit from the analysis. That is why I tried to describe what I did and said and what the children did and said and give details about the context of the sessions (Merriam, 1995; Noble & Smith, 2015; Shenton, 2004). This attitude towards the transferability of this qualitative research and its writing up was necessary for another reason, too; its comparative character. To me, this means that I must remind the reader of differences and similarities between the education provision for five year olds in Greece and Scotland, so as to stop readers as well as myself (for the qualitative and comparative aspect of the study) from misinterpreting data based on the readers' knowledge of one of the two education systems or mine.

In addressing the trustworthiness of this research, I need to state that I accept and agree with Sandelowski's (1993) understanding that dependability threatens credibility. I, too, think that ensuring dependability in the sense that the findings of a qualitative research can be repeated at different time points or places or by different researchers (Denzin & Lincoln, 1994, as cited in Cohen, Manion, & Morrison, 2018) goes against the nature and purpose of qualitative studies. A qualitative study aims at recording, analyzing and understanding the multiplicity of reality so repeatability (which dependability entails) is not a feature of priority when investigating qualitatively (Cohen, Manion, & Morrison, 2018; Hatch, 1995). When taking a qualitative approach to research, as I tried to do, generalizability is not the issue. As Patrick Hughes (2001, p. 53) writes 'qualitative research is concerned with the quality of the data it produces rather than just its quantity'.

Discussing confirmability (Lincoln & Guba, 1985), Noble and Smith (2015) expand on reflexivity; they emphasize that it is ensured by the researcher stating their views on the subject they are studying and trying to consciously separate their views from those of the participants, which I tried to do, too. I agree with Jans (2004) in that cultural and social class factors do affect children's lives and as a result the education they are offered and experience. In the same vein, these factors do the same to a researcher and I am conscious of that influence. I need to explain that I have lived only in Europe, so my worldview, which influences my thinking about children and analyzing my data is European (or even Eurocentric), Christian, of a white, middle-aged female in a patriarchal society, of a single mother from a poor family and a teacher with all her official education on young children's education. Based on that, I do not and cannot claim generalizability to all children everywhere, only to the children who we were kind enough to help me and from my perspective on young children and their education, which follows.

I start with my distrust towards the meaning of the term 'human' in the Convention of the right of the child and in what it means to be a member of the human family (Preamble of the Convention). In my mother tongue, Greek, the words human and man are one; it is Anthropos[8]. There is a problem with the word anthropos in terms of sexism because grammatically it is masculine gender, which excludes half of the species but then again so many words function like that in Greek. Also in Greek, words like humanity, humanism, humane, humanitarian, inhuman, subhuman, man, mankind and superman derive from the word anthropos and there are not two words (human and man) to describe people, as it happens in English.

So, on the one hand, I see the term chattel which describes a man, a woman and a child, *i.e.* human beings, as property and thus as non-human or less human or subhuman. On the other hand, there are still people who live like chattel or slaves with the original meaning of the terms and not just as people exploited in terms of pay. Therefore, there is scope for the term human which applies to children to be abused. What I mean is that the word human in the term human rights is not enough without it being defined and accompanied by complimentary and equally clearly defined, unambiguous attributes of what constitutes a member of the human family. Consequently, I have concerns about the potential abuse of the term 'human dignity' in its interpretation in general as well as when it comes to children. Furthermore, I think that the above potential for multiple interpretations of the terms human (and its derivatives) and dignity is also relevant to the position and place of children in the family of humans.

I believe that children are capable of many more things and that they can act a lot more autonomously and rationally than traditional developmental psychology in Europe supports (Walkerdine, 1998; Woodhead, 1999). I accept them as my coequals in the sense that they are beings and becomings of mankind, just like me, and simultaneously different from me in the same way as the rest of the people are and not just because they are young, not just because of their age. Children may have less experiences than me (*e.g.* in terms perhaps of education, employment, children of their own) but they have different experiences from me, too. The experiences some children have I did not have as a child (*e.g.* computers, mobile phones, access to virtual reality, playgroups and a variety of playthings) but then there are other children who do not have the experiences I had as a child (*e.g.* food, clean water, shelter, healthcare, family, school) half a century ago. So, children experience their early years with many visible differences from how I did but that is something that happens with all other people on the planet, whether they are children now or my age now.

I think that five to six year old children's perception of *their rights* and of themselves as *right holders* as these terms are legally defined is limited or even non-existent, depending on the culture they are brought up in and the contact and experience children have with such terminology and practices (*e.g.* Ruck, Keating, Abramovitch, & Koegl, 1998, as cited in Covell & Howe, 2001). In this sense, I accept that children need to be taught about their rights and develop skills necessary to claim them (article 5 of the Convention) but then again so do many adults in different places of the world. Even those who can and know how to exercise their rights have learned about them and were allowed to learn and exercise them.

Furthermore, I believe that even the youngest of children have some sense of right and wrong, of justice (which I believe may vary according to the culture they live in and the contact children have with terminology and discussions on such matters) and of what is good for them in terms of education, for example. I also believe that even the youngest of children can tell or show other people if what they experience is bad for them, harms them or if it is good for them and at age five to six even partly explain their reasons for some of their views.

I do not think that young children consider themselves *equal to adults,* that is, same in size, ability and status [9] and that is why they try all means (*e.g.* tantrums, whining) available to them in their culture to make adults do or give more of whatever they deny or forbid children to do or have (see also Sevón, 2015; Singer, 1996). In my opinion, this happens because this is something they are taught about themselves. It also happens because children understand that their bodies are too small or not so strong for some of the everyday natural or societal experiences they have (a world made by adults for adults or even a world made by some white men for some white men) and that is why they need adults to protect them or provide for them at times. This is one part of children's agency in my opinion, *i.e.* they can exert some influence over matters taking place around them which interest them, since other more adult-like or dignified ways are not always allowed or taught to them. However, they learn how to exercise their agency more frequently and efficiently when they are involved and participate in decision making processes and in social life in general (see also Sirkko, Kyrönlampi, & Puroila, 2019; Stoecklin, 2012).

I also agree with Quennerstedt and Quennerstedt (2014) in that school cannot accomplish its purpose if children are considered only as becomings and not as beings simultaneously, and I think that this applies to schooling in early childhood, too. Each society has schools to teach children information and develop skills in them regardless of whether we all agree as to whose information and whose skills are included and excluded and how useful all of these really are to all children. As I have already shown, I believe in the influence of the culture one experiences, regardless of whether they are an adult or a child, as well as in the influence of society, economy, politics, natural environment, education, and historical point in time on people. Similarly, I believe that not all cultures, national, dominant or other, allow for the development of all the potential in children that the Convention acknowledges for them, such their being dignified and quite capable and reasonable people. Furthermore, I do not believe that it is only lack of knowledge about their rights and how to exercise them that hinders children, as well as older people, from exercising more agency (see also Jones & Welsh, 2018; Sevón, 2015). I believe that, in the same way adult citizens are not consulted by their governments about issues affecting them, so are children. Consequently, I do not believe that children have a culture of their own that is so distant from that of the adults (see also Lancy, 2012) nor that a culture is always a constraint to people or a constraint only to children.

NOTES

[1] Scotland is part of the United Kingdom in the Hofstede's options of countries to compare.

[2] Dominant culture is the group of people who 'generally exercises the greatest influence on the beliefs, values, perceptions, communication patterns, and customs of the culture' (Samovar, Porter, McDaniel, & Roy, 2013, p. 8).

[3] Co-cultures are 'groups or social communities exhibiting perceptions, values, beliefs, communicative behaviors, and social practices that are sufficiently different as to distinguish them from other groups and communities and from the dominant culture' (Samovar, Porter, McDaniel, & Roy, 2013, p. 9).

[4] Children are some of the less powerful groups in any society.

[5] Or were forced to know.

[6] We cannot compare apples to pears, as Clarkson (2009) explains.

[7] Streaming was practiced in both primary schools in Scotland but in none of the kindergartens in Greece. It is not practiced at all in Greek state run schools.

[8] Ἄνθρωπος.

[9] Someone who is your equal has the same ability, status, or rights as you have (Collins Dictionary, 2021).

CHAPTER 4

Children's Views about an Authoritarian School

Abstract: In this chapter, the data produced in the first focus group session with children in Scotland and Greece are analyzed. The children who participated in this session were read the plan for a teacher-directed school for young children, which does not provide for most of the children's rights relevant to their education. Children in both countries mainly talked about the physical environment of the school in the plan, which they found poor and hindering play (article 31). In terms of the social environment of the authoritarian school, children wanted to be consulted (article 12) but this tendency was stronger in Scotland and only children from Greece talked about the need for children to be safe at school (article 19). The significance of article 5 on adults helping children with exercising their rights was raised.

Keywords: Children's participation, Right to education, Right to play, Right to protection from physical harm, Teacher-directed school.

INTRODUCTION

Children in both countries were given the following plan for a school intended to be the best school ever.

In this school, the teacher will make all the decisions for the children. She will set the classroom rules for the children without asking them and she will punish them when they do not follow them. The teacher will prepare lessons for the children and all of them will do the same thing at the same time. All the children will sit quietly and listen to their teacher. When there is a break, the teacher will let the children play for a while. Then she will stop them and start her lesson again. Around the school there will be a high wire netting. The yard will be small, covered in cement and have a few trees. Inside the school we will put rows of desks, a blackboard, a clock on the wall and a large desk for the teacher.

Since they did not agree that it was a plan for a perfect school, they were asked for suggestions to improve it. The first thing children from both groups in Scotland and from two of the three groups from Greece mentioned referred to the physical environment, even though it is described last in the plan. Only the children in one group in Greece did not let me tell them the whole plan and then discuss it. They commented on the first element of the plan as I was reading, so I accepted a discussion on one element of the plan after another.

The Physical Environment of a School

Scotland

There were two groups of children, one from Valley primary school and one from Hill primary school in Scotland who discussed an authoritarian school for children of their age. The first thing children in both groups in Scotland mentioned as improvement of the plan of a perfect school for five year olds was about play. Contact with nature at school was also important to these groups. Only girls participated in the focus groups of both schools.

Valley School

More time for play and more space for play in the yard as well as contact with flora (*e.g.* sunflowers) were important to the plan of the best school, together with an element of academic school structure, such as a bell.

ES: So, I was wondering, can you help the queen and the king make the best school ever? Do you think this plan is the best or have you got any other ideas?

We can have a longer play time.

We could have a bigger playground.

And not covered in cement.

ES: Not covered in cement. What would you like on the floor on the yard?

Hmm ... Probably a few flowers.

ES: Flowers! Grass? Trees?

We could put some more ... we could put trees on the grass.

ES: Alright. Anything else to make this school they want to build better?

Maybe have a bell so that they know when it is break time and stuff?

ES: A bell.

We can have a sunflower.

ES: A sunflower. Plant sunflowers?

Cause the sunflowers in our garden are dying.

ES: Alright. Anything else?

Nope.

These children answers indicate the importance of article 31, that is, children right to rest, leisure and play, and of article 28.1. about children's s rights to education. Children would add a bell to the plan so that children know when teaching ends and children can have a break. A bell in a primary school is a feature of a school found in primary schools in both countries. However, children aged five to six are in kindergartens in Greece and a tambourine is used to signal the change from a teacher directed activity to child directed activity and vise versa. These children did not reject the idea of learning in school and indicated how important it was for children to know what activities follow; to know the daily routine. Children suggestions for a bell show that children may not know how to tell time or how to estimate the duration of activities and that they were not involved in, or perhaps not even informed of, how long each activity takes in class. Article 29(e), which refers to children being taught to respect the natural environment at school, seems to have a strong basis of being implemented successfully, as these children were interested in flora [1].

Hill School

Children in the group from Hill School also commented on the physical environment of the best school ever in terms of play resources (seesaw, climbing frame, *etc.*), space for play and contact with flora (flower garden). However, their emphasis on play equipment was stronger compared to that from the Valley School, because they described more resources for play. They also made provisions to ensure the potential to rest (big bed) and eat (lunch boxes) in the classroom exists in the physical environment of a perfect school.

ES: So, can you help her [the queen] make the best school ever? Do you have any ideas?

Make a shoot for them?

ES: What do you mean, a shoot?

Make a slide.

ES: Anything else?

Make a roundabout.

A flower garden.

A seesaw.

And a track with go carts to drive in.

A swing.

ES: Alright, swing.

Ladders to get up on the shoot.

Climbing frame.

A mirror.

ES: A mirror? Where? In the classroom?

In the classroom.

ES: A mirror. Ok. Anything else in the classroom?

I'd like to have a play house.

A library.

ES: A library? Anything else?

Bed.

ES: A bed. For you? For the dolls?

For everyone.

ES: For everyone. So, both for the toys and the children.

Yeah.

ES: So how big is this going to be?

Master.

Big size.

ES: Big size. Ok. A big one. Like the ones you have at home or like the ones your moms and dads have at home?

Moms and dads'.

ES: Moms and dads', right.

As big as this, as this library[2].

Yeah.

That is how big it's going to be. But it's going to be tall.

ES: How tall?

Up to the ceiling.

ES: How are you going to get up on the bed if it's up to the ceiling?

Ladders.

ES: Ladders? Ok.

A lunchbox in the classroom.

ES: Lunch boxes in the classroom.

In case you get hungry.

And a play jungle.

ES: Where?

Outside.

And a soft play.

ES: What's a soft play?

It's something for inside but you can have it outside, if you want, and it's like a play area.

Yeah.

ES: So, it's something that you can have in the classroom and then you can move *it outside and play it outside?*

Yeah.

Bouncing castle.

And you have to take your shoes off.

ES: For the bouncing castle?

Yeah, for the soft play and the bouncing castle.

And a jungle venture.

Maybe some teddies?

ES: Teddies?

Teddy bears.

Yeah, I like teddy bears.

And some fruit.

ES: Fruit?

I already said some lunch box.

ES: Lunch boxes and fruit. So, you want to eat in the classroom. Ok.

This is making feel so tired and hungry that I just want to go to bed and eat something.

Some chairs?

New chairs.

Pink chairs.

Oh, and a table!

Pink tables as well.

ES: Tables.

Glittery tables.

And glittery pink chairs.

With sparkles on them.

Later, children in Hill School added even more materials to the plan for the new school. They wanted animals in school, access to iPads and televisions, less restrictions on their play and permission to bring things from home to school.

ES: Anything else you want to say to the queen about her problem?

How many TVs?

ES: She doesn't have any TVs.

We don't have TVs. We don't watch TV in school.

ES: Would you like to have the choice to watch TV in school?

Yeah.

Yeah.

Yeah.

I could watch 'Prince Paul' and 'Painting with Mary'[3].

I wish animals could come and we could touch them.

Or we could just bring to school whatever you have at home?

Ipads?

ES: Alright, bring Ipads to school, too.

We could play whatever we like.

ES: Like what? Whatever you like, like what?

Toys and books and stuff like that.

The children views are in accordance with article 31 on their right to play and leisure as they asked for a more child-centered and lax environment in school (*e.g.* watching television, eating and resting in classroom) rather than a purely academically centered one. It is also noteworthy that iPads and books were included as items to play with together with toys. This suggests that iPads and books are resources not only used by teachers to teach but resources these children perceived as necessary for child initiated activities. Such a perception is in accordance with article 17 of the Convention on the children right to access information and article 28.1 and their right to education. Children had an interest in nature both as flora and as fauna, so, there was an interest which can be used by teachers as a basis for developing children respect for the natural environment in accordance with article 29(e).

Greece

Three groups coming from three different kindergartens in Greece respectively were read the plan for an authoritarian school. Two out of the three groups discussed space for play, even though all groups would add play resources, which would require more physical space. Children also referred to their right to physical safety (article 19) and, through mentioning their contact with nature at school, to their right to education (article 29(e)). Only the children from Pine School did not link nature to the physical environment of a school. All three groups in Greece included both girls and boys.

Elm School

These children's primary concern was children's safety while playing, which, in their view, was not provided by trees and cement in the school yard of the plan they were read. They preferred flowers to trees and grass to cement and a large school yard. Play at first seemed to come last in their suggestions but they soon expanded on more resources for play and more space for play. These children related the teacher's role, in terms of discipline and setting standards of appropriate behavior in school (but not of learning) to the physical environment. They involved the teacher's reaction to the unsafe yard of the plan and talked about rules on appropriate behavior towards each other, too. This group considered that a teacher is to mediate and thus teach them how to behave towards their classmates.

ES: *So, what do you think? Is this the plan for the best school ever?*

No.

ES: So, tell me what you do not like about it.

I do not like that it has trees and cement because, if a child runs into a tree, they will fall and hurt themselves. And the rest of the children, if they do not respect them[4] , they will be told off by the teacher and I would not like it.

Me neither.

Me neither.

ES: Anything else you do not like about this school?

I do not like it that the teacher would tell them off.

Me, too.

ES: Any other ideas?

I do not like the plan they thought of.

I'd like that they cut down the trees to make a yard.

ES: They did not say that. They said that the yard would have some trees but not many.

I would prefer they thought of cutting down the trees and made them into benches.

ES: Okay. Then what do we keep from this plan and what do we change?

Let's change the tree and cement parts.

Let's change the teacher's scolding.

Let's change the plan they thought about this school.

ES: What do we change?

To have a play house, a chair and a desk.

Let's make the plan different. Let's have a large yard.

They can have tables and their teacher not scolding them. She could just talk to the children about not fighting and (about) being together.

And not to have trees and cement. Let's change the cement into grass and let's change trees into flowers.

Or we can cut them and make seats out of them.

Let's have a big desk[5], a teacher that does not tell children off, who has a child apologise when they hit another, say thank you and please. And who has children quiet and not told off.

There is some danger. So, not to have furniture that are pointy because children may hurt themselves.

ES: Do you think the furniture is dangerous?

Some of it is. Somebody may hurt themselves at this corner[6]."

These children views reflect their rights as described in (a) articles 28.1 and 29(e) on children right to education, which develops respect for nature in school among other things, (b) article 31 on children right to play and leisure and (c) article 19 on children right to safety and protection from physical harm. They also agree with article 6(c) of the GC 2005, which expresses that children in their relationships with other children 'learn to negotiate and coordinate shared activities, resolve conflicts, keep agreements and accept responsibility for others'.

Therefore, in this new school the teacher would set rules about children respecting each other (*e.g.* not laughing at each other when they fall), would teach them how to treat others (*e.g.* not hitting others) and would teach them manners (*e.g.* saying thank you). They seemed to accept these roles for a teacher but not her intense, in their view, reaction when children disobeyed rules. They preferred a teacher who does not scold children but resorts to talking, as children did not want to be talked to angrily when they misbehaved. Scolding was perceived as not appropriate treatment of children's disobedience. Their views about children misbehavior echo article 29(b) which explains that the education of children is to be directed towards respect for human rights and article 28.2., which explains that school discipline should respect children dignity and their rights. The children views also reflected the Preamble of the Convention, since they did not want one to laugh at another, but to respect their dignity.

Oak School

Unlike Elm School, children in Oak School focused on equipping the school with toys and other play resources for the indoors (play corners[7]) and for the outdoors e.g. swings, seesaws, slides, roundabouts, puzzles, toys, robots) and as well as with fauna e.g. dogs, bees, butterflies and wasps). Flora was mentioned, too, but children in Oak School did not consider trees dangerous, like children in Elm School did.

ES: Well, around the school yard there will be high wire netting. The yard will not be large and it will be covered in cement and have a few trees.

No, I wouldn't like it.

ES: So, tell us what does the perfect school yard look like?

We should put some toys in, let's put a slide.

Swings.

Seesaw.

Have grass.

A roundabout.

Have flowers.

ES: What else would you like in the yard?

Wood sorrels.

ES: What are the wood sorrels?

Flowers. They have yellow petals and some people chew them and spit them. But you can make them a salad.

ES: Anything else you would like in the perfect school yard?

I would like for it to have butterflies.

Bees and wasps.

ES: If you have flowers, they will come.

Animals.

ES: Animals? What animals?

Puppy dogs.

But in most schools, animals are not allowed.

ES: You can have classroom pets like hamsters or little mice.

We have dinosaurs.

ES: Alive ones?

No, toys.

ES: So, do you want to have some of them in the yard?

Yes.

ES: So, let me tell you the last part of the plan. They wanted to build a classroom with desks in it for the children, a big desk for the teacher, a board and a clock.

Sounds good to me.

ES: Without corners.

Oh, no.

Perhaps the teacher would also have a stick and when children get in the room, she may hit them with it.

That would suck!

ES: How would the perfect school be? What would you put in it?

Toys.

ES: What toys?

Toy animals, puzzles, painting, brushes.

A toy kitchen.

Books.

A toy where we can tinker on[8].

Toy robots.

Transformers.

A balcony.

The views of this group reflect the importance of article 31 on the children right to play. These children linked school, and by default their education, with nature (fauna and flora), which facilitates the cultivation of respect for the natural environment in children and is in accordance with article 29(e). They also referred briefly to children's physical protection from an abusive teacher, so, article 19 was important to them.

Pine School

Children in this group added resources for the perfect school. They clearly stated they wanted more space for play and more toys. Tables, benches, and chairs, which can be used both in teacher-initiated learning activities as well as child-initiated activities, were also mentioned.

ES: Is this the best school?

No.

Why not?

Because the yard is small.

Because it is too small.

ES: Would children like it?

No, because children would get stuck!

ES: So, should it be larger?

It should be larger! Much larger! Like ours!

ES: And what else should this school have?

Toys.

ES: What toys would you like?

Like the ones we have.

Toy fruit.

Shops (a play area).

Hair dresser's (a play area).

Clothes [for dress up].

And Legos.

And mats.

And toy tools.

And little tables.

And little chairs like this one.

And benches.

Therefore, for these children, the implementation of article 28.1, of their right to an education was a priority. Their reference to benches, tables and chairs, which can be used both in teacher-directed and child-directed activities, indicates the importance of article 29(a) especially in terms of education developing 'the child's personality, talents and mental and physical activities' and of article 31 on children right to play.

Comparison of Children's Perspectives on the Physical Environment

Children in both countries linked the physical environment of the best school ever to articles 28, 29 and 31, which refer to children right to education and play. That is so, because they suggested both toys and resources which can be used both for teacher-initiated and children-initiated activities. Such an example is a library and its books, which can be used by children either at the request of their teachers or because children want to read.

Children in Valley School in Scotland wanted a larger playground and more time for play, whereas in Greece children from Pine School wanted more space both indoors and outdoors but did not mention anything relevant to time for play. The rest of the children from both countries only mentioned more resources for play and rest, some of which were large in size, such as big beds, and bouncy castles, or would require a lot of space to have them, such as flowers and animals. So, even though they did not link resources to space, it can be inferred that so many things, flora and fauna would require a bigger building and a bigger yard.

Children in Scotland did not connect the physical environment of the authoritarian school to their right to safety (article 19), unlike some children in Greece. Across Greece, there were differences in terms of perceiving safety from physical harm (article 19) in the school yard in Elm School and in terms of discussing teachers' behavior which ensures safety for children in Elm School or jeopardizes it in Oak School. The group from Elm School linked safety to the work of the teacher who was supposed to *legislate* for the protection of children from harm. Children in Oak School did not want a teacher who may hit children, even though the word punishment was used in the plan for an authoritarian school. Their views about the role of a teacher echoed not only article 19 but article 28.2., which emphasizes the administration of discipline in a way that respects children dignity.

The Social Environment of A School

Scotland

When it comes to the children's part in setting the rules at school and in decision making, children in Scotland were interested in being consulted by their teachers, in talking about matters with their teachers, indicating that in fact, they did not as much as they wanted.

Valley School

This group wanted children to be consulted by the teacher of the improved plan for a school, but for a small number of rules at a time or in small groups of children.

ES: In this school the teacher will make all the rules. Not the children. She will not ask the children. How do you feel about that?

Sad?

ES: Sad. How do you think it will be better? Should she ask the children?

Yeah. She could ask one group at a time.

ES: Alright she could ask the children in small groups about the rules. Do you think she should ask children about all the rules? Or some ...

No.

Yeah.

ES: Ok. Can you explain yourselves one at a time? So, Kathy, you said yes. She should ask the children about all the rules?

Because if the teacher ignores someone, then they wouldn't know what to do, maybe?

ES: Because if the teacher ignored them?

Yeah.

ES: Ignore what? The children?

When someone fell over.

No one helped them.

ES: Ok, this is a rule. So, she should ... the teacher should ask the children about all the rules?

Yeah.

ES: Why? Can you repeat it?

Because someone may fall over and she doesn't want to help them.

ES: Alright. If somebody falls over and the other children don't help.
So, it's better if everybody knows, is asked about the rules. Ok. And you, Lilly, you said that she shouldn't ask all the children about all the rules. What do you mean?

She could ask some persons about the rules.

ES: Alright.

She could do some rules at a time.

ES: Ok. So, you say she should ask them about all the rules, but not all at once. Just for a few rules at a time. Ok.

These children referred to certain rules that had to do with helping others when they are not safe or when they do not know what to do. Their views reflected the importance of article 19 about children safety to this group. They also indicated that children wanted to be consulted when decisions affecting them, such as rules of behavior, are being made (article 12). However, they wanted to do this in a manner suited to their abilities, such as discussing and thinking about a few rules at a time or one rule at a time before decisions are made. Article 5 and a need for guidance in the implementation of their rights on the teachers' part was expressed by this group.

Children were also asked directly about how they felt about children in the plan not deciding anything with their teachers. They expressed their sadness towards children not being allowed to decide about anything and not having choices.

ES: You know in this school the teacher will decide about everything. Everything that happens. How do you feel about that?

Sad?

Yeah, sad.

ES: Why? Why is that?

Because then the teacher tells us everything, what to do. And then no one else gets to have choices. Some decisions.

Yeah.

So, these children wanted a school, which allowed children some initiative. They did not indicate that they wanted to do something different on the basis of their being children. On the contrary, they wanted to be able to do what older people do, that is, pick and choose about some topics. They did not speak like children whose nature in this matter is different from the adults. Later I asked:

ES: If you could decide things with your teacher, what would you like to decide with her?

I would decide with my teacher to pick some more flowers then.

ES: You mean in the garden or in the classroom?

In the classroom.

Maybe we could do some craft and painting.

ES: Anything else you would like to decide with her?

No.

Children expressed their wanting to have nature (*i.e.* flowers) in the classroom, which perhaps indicates a sense of beauty and aesthetics. This was also expressed in their wanting to do painting and some crafts, which can be relevant to arts. So, more nature and more making things with one's hands were aspects of school they would like to decide about with their teachers. These topics of decision fall into the directions of education as defined in the paragraphs of article 29. Paragraph (a) of article 29 defines an education that develops their [children's] talents and potential and paragraph (e) an education that cultivates children's respect for the natural environment.

Hill School

The girls in this group said that the teacher should not set all the rules on her own and that they did not want children to be bossed around by the teacher in the plan. There was, however, one girl who said that there were no bad rules. She added that children needed rules on safety and that it is somehow alright for the teacher to make rules. The role of the teacher as a protector of children from their peers was important.

ES: The plan says that the teacher will make all the classroom rules. How do you feel about that?

It would be bossy.

And a little bit ok.

ES: And a little bit ok. In what way?

Umm ...

ES: Why did you say it would be ok?

There are no bad rules.

ES: Well, what if she made some rules you didn't like, would you tell her?

We need some rules so that we don't hit each other or push each other.

ES: What would you do? Would you tell the teacher? Would you tell the teacher that you didn't like the rules?

Yeah.

Yeah.

And what would you expect? What would you want?

A new classroom.

ES: A new classroom.

A new teacher.

And a new school.

ES: And a new school. Ok.

Children in this group believed that a teacher should consult children about setting the class rules (article 12) but one of them believed that a teacher could not do wrong with her rules, even if she does not consult children. This girl thought that rules about acceptable behavior were perhaps something for the adults to, at least, set an example. Her view seemed to echo article 12 and the importance of article 5. She was torn between children being consulted (article 12) but also being guided by teachers in exercising their rights (article 5). The girls mentioned only one rule, which was children being stopped from harming one another. So, teachers were there to clarify and ensure that all children are to be protected from other children (article 19).

This group were not in favour of a teacher deciding everything in school and they raised the extreme example of children being told what game to play by their teacher.

ES: How would you feel if you were in school and the teacher decided about everything?

Not good.

Not good.

ES: *If you had to ask her about every move you made?*

If she at a play time "You'll have to play hide and seek", that's a bit bossy.

ES: *Bossy. Ok.*

Children wanted the plan to allow children some freedom and not to lead them to asking the teacher for permission all the time. I took the discussion to a more personal level and directly asked them about decisions in their school.

ES: *Do you want to make decisions with your teachers in school?*

Yeah.

ES: *Decisions about what?*

Toys.

About choices.

Toys.

ES: *Toys. Ok, so, you want to decide with your teachers about toys and choices. What else?*

Can we have butterflies in school?

Umm, bunnies.

ES: *If you can have bunnies in school.*

And butterflies.

ES: *So you said you want to decide with your teachers, about your toys, about the little animals you want to have in school, what else?*

I wish we could play on the computer.

ES: *So, you want to decide with your teacher ...*

If we can play on the computer.

I wish we could go to sleep.

ES: *Alright, you want to sleep but you're in school.*

Yeah.

Yeah.

Alright.

ES: *Do you want to sleep after lunch?*

No.

Yeah.

No.

I wish we could sleep whenever we want.

I wish I could sleep all the time.

ES: *So, you want to decide with your teacher about some things, like if you're going to sleep in school or what you are going to do in school.*

Yeah.

And I wish they had fairy costumes and mermaid costumes.

Yeah.

And you could make all the mermaid costumes in school.

Me, too.

I do.

I do.

I don't.

This group wanted children to decide about matters with their teachers (article 12) as an improvement of the plan for a school. When discussing topics for decision-making with their teachers, they, too, wanted nature in school but in the form of animals and not flowers as in Valley School. Such a view forms a strong basis for the implementation of article 29(e) and teaching children to respect the natural environment. Toys, in general, clothes for dress-up play, and computer games were necessary as well as children being able to sleep whenever they wanted. So, this group wanted more contact with nature (article 29(e)), more play and more rest (article 31) to be added to the plan of the authoritarian school they were read but they themselves could not decide about such matters with their teacher.

Greece

In Greece, most of the children were in favor of a teacher consulting with children about rules as a change in the plan for a school best for children their age. Only children from Elm School were adamant that it was not the children's place to set the classroom rules or share the setting of rules with their teacher. When it comes to participation in decision making, only children in Oak School believed that teachers know what is best for them but that they should tell children their decisions in a respectful manner. The rest of them wanted to be consulted about decisions affecting them.

Elm School

Children in this group did not believe in teachers consulting with children about school rules. They agreed with the idea of teachers setting the rules for children expressed in the plan.

ES: Let me ask you another thing. The plan says that the teacher will make all the classroom rules without asking the children. Do you agree?

Yes, because the teacher must set the rules.

Because children, without learning the rules, do not know many [rules] and we ourselves do not know that many [rules]. But our teacher does most of the things.

According to this group, teachers in school are supposed do most of the things that take place. One of the things teachers are to do in school is to set the classroom rules because children do not know many rules and they must learn some. Consultation or co-decision about rules is not a thing that these children believe in, so the implementation of article 12 was not an issue for them. They believed that children do not know how to act and behave in school and so their teachers were to show them how. Therefore, they could not recognize their potential, their evolving capacities and their ability to contribute to rule formation. Perhaps they had internalized that they were not able to respond to such a task or even being taught about it, which the children from Valley School believed. Such views are very likely an example of what the low score in individualism in Greece (Hofstede, 2021b) means in relation to the implementation of article 12 at school. It means that in such a culture, children owe allegiance to the community they belong to and protects them and are delayed in making decisions on their own. This group's views emphasize the significance of article 5 in relation to the implementation of article 12. Children views indicated that they needed direction and guidance 'to compensate for their lack of knowledge and experience' (article 84 of GC 12, 2009), if they were to act according to their rights. However, if their teacher did most things in their class, then she sounds a lot like the teacher of the plan, which explains why children did not reject the idea.

On the other hand, this group believed in children making decisions with their teachers in general and vague terms. They did not express any feelings about it but mentioned ethics in terms of right and wrong.

ES: The plan says that the teacher will decide about everything. How do you feel about that?

No, the teacher should not decide on her own.

No, this is not right, both adults and children should decide together.

The children in this group stressed the importance of article 12 when they were asked about sharing decisions with their teachers about matters other than rule setting. When asked what they wanted to decide with their teachers, the topics of decisions were more like suggestions to improve their own school, so, more like wanting their views to be considered by their teachers. They wanted different colors on the walls, different tables and a larger yard with toys. They wanted more contact with the children of the adjacent primary school. Space, color, toys and company with children were features they thought their school needed and thus matters they wanted to decide about with their teachers. Furthermore, they saw their teacher as the appropriate person to be a mediator for them to be granted the changes their school needs rather than the one who decides and does what she thinks best, unlike children in Scotland who presented their teachers as more distant.

ES: What would you like to decide with your teachers?

I would tell my teacher to change something on the walls, to paint them. To rebuild the school more nicely because if some children do not pay attention to the furniture, they bump into them. The teacher can tell the king and the queen to paint the wall, to demolish it and rebuild it.

ES: Yes, I see what you mean.

We will get round tables and paint the walls yellow.

It will be a little larger.

ES: What would you like larger? A larger yard, larger classrooms?

A larger yard.

ES: And what else would this yard have? Will it have anything else?

Tramboline.

Slide.

I would like it (the new school) to have a larger yard, a roundabout, space to run. We want it to have toys and to share our breaks with the children of the primary school and all of us to be friends.

But the school should be colourful because if it has one colour, it will not look very colourful.

To have a seesaw too, the yard to have a seesaw too!

Children in Elm School discussed the queen and king's plan in relation to the shortcomings of the physical environment of their own kindergarten. Actually, most of their suggestions were school shortcomings because of the limited budgets. These did not allow teachers to paint schools or buy new tables. The particular school had a really small yard for so many children, therefore, there was not much space for play equipment as well as money to buy it. So, children reasonably suggested a higher, rich authority to provide these; the queen and king. Their suggestions meant that they understood that the problems requiring a solution in the form of a decision for improvement was not something their teachers did not allow. They wanted to be consulted, as article 12 foresees, but they believed that their issues could not be solved by decisions made by them with their teachers. This was the only group, out of the five who were read the plan for an authoritarian school in both countries, who linked participation with national legislation in accordance with articles 128-9 of GC 12 2009. They were also the only ones who linked article 12 to article 6(c) of the GC 7 2005 on the relationships with other older children as a feature of early childhood (from birth to 8 years) and in a way to article 15 on the children right of freedom of association. This practice of not allowing older children in the same school yard as younger ones has been recorded by others, such as Sirkko, Kyronlaampi, and Puroila (2019) in Finland and was true for Hill School in Scotland, which had a nursery class.

Oak School

Children from Oak School wanted the teacher of the school plan to consult with the children in her class instead of setting the rules on her own. Their reply sounds a lot like the one given by the children in Hill School from Scotland who said that they would leave their school if the teacher set the rules on her own. It indicates that their right to be heard (article 12) was so important to them that its violation in school would make them leave it.

ES: Like I said the plan says that the teacher will make all the classroom rules without asking the children. How do you feel about that?

No, she must listen to the children's views.

Yes, because otherwise nobody would want to go to school, the school would be empty.

ES: So, if your teacher asked you to talk about your rules, what would you say to her?

We in our class have set rules and we use a little worm[9] which shows them all.

We, too, have written what we should do.

ES: Would you like to add a rule or erase one?

Erase one.

ES: Which one?

About not sommersaulting.

ES: In the classroom? Why don't your teachers let you do sommersaults?

Because we may hurt ourselves.

But I know how to sommersault.

ES: How about the rest of you? Any other rules you would add or omit?

If we had a few toys in our classroom, we could bring some [from home] in or give away some toys.

Only one child wanted a rule revoked, even though I find it dangerous. Even if she could sommersault, her classroom was not that large, others may come too close to her, move furniture, *etc.* and cause an accident. So, this child is interested in her gratification but not in her safety or the safety of others in accordance with article 19. Another rule children in this group wanted to add to the plan was to be allowed to enrich the toys in the kindergarten with their toys from home. Play (article 31) was important to them as well as their school and education (article 28.1).

When asked about decision making, this group mentioned the class president and that children's views should be considered by the teacher rather than children being instructed to do something. They did not link the question to their free play time.

ES: Well, the queen and king's helpers advised them to build a school where the teacher would decide everything.

No.

So, you do not like it. George[10] , what do you think? Is this a good idea so as to make the best school ever?

No.

ES: What must the teacher do to make the best school ever?

We should ask her[11] [if they are allowed to do something] and she should tell us what to do. Not just tell us what to do.

Doesn't each class have a class president?

ES: Yes. George is talking about the children president, that is a child who the rest of the children voted in order to talk to the teachers and headteachers.

We voted for one in our class[12].

However, the discussion ended there, the children could not elaborate more on the topic. Anyway, what else could they have said as presidency in kindergarten is a tokenistic, honorary title (Arnstein, 1969; Cornwall, 2008) with no jurisdiction? Children in this group mentioned only (a) that they want to be respected enough to be asked by their teacher about issues concerning them and (b) that they knew that their teacher would know the answer. Such views could be an indication of what the low score in individualism in Greece (Hofstede 2021b) means in relation to the implementation of article 12 at school. It is a suggestion that brings out the need for the implementation of article 5 according to which children have a right to direction and guidance to compensate for children's lack of knowledge and experience and their still evolving capacities (see also article 84 in GC 12, 2009). It raises the importance of article 5 so that children can exercise their rights and, in this case, article 12.

Pine School

Two of the children in this group mentioned that the teacher must set the rules, then another said the teacher should consult the children and then they started talking about how oppressed they felt by the rules in their class. They appeared to dislike not being able to change the position of furniture and apparatuses indoors. This suggests that once space was determined by teachers there were no negotiations or consultations about it, which agrees with the high score of power distance in Greece. So, indirectly I was given to understand that children wanted to be consulted about rules in a way because they did not agree with the rule 'children do not move furniture to play or have fun in the classroom'. However, there are authors who consider allowing children to change the limits of the various play areas if it helps them to continue or develop their play, as part of a pedagogy of play (Wood, 2010).

The intensity of this oppression was such that they even suggested smashing up the classroom. It appears that they were restricted to their classroom when indoors, and simultaneously were curious about resources in other classrooms. They also wanted to have more time with other children, even after opening hours, and more time for play.

ES: Do you want her to ask you about the rules of the class?

No.

ES: No? Should the teacher decide them?

Yes.

Yes.

No, she should ask us, too.

I wish there were no rules.

ES: If there were no rules, what would you do that you cannot do now?

We would do silly little things.

ES: Silly little things like what?

I would push the table, pull the chair.

I would come in and sit here and play. I would put the table out of the room.

I would get it out in the yard and get on it.

And we would remove the blankets.

And I would take a bench in the circle time area and put the TV there and turn on the TV to watch all day and night and do whatever I want.

And at night we would come here [to school] and lie down and sleep. What do you think?

Yes, to unfold the blankets.

Maybe we can go to other classrooms to see their things and play with whichever we like.

We want to play day and night.

We would invite all the girls in here to play.

And all the boys.

No.

Yes. All the boys, too. And we will smash up the place.

And to bring all the things that break from home and break them.

Except for the toys because we like them.

Even though the conversation was about rules, the children indicated how important play was to them and how much they wanted more time to spend on play with their peers. However, both play and time with other children were related to school, thus emphasizing the importance of both article 28.1 and article 31 to them. Children wanted to be with other children in school not only for the time their teachers had to keep them there but for longer as if school was a place for children to associate with each other (article 15) and not only for children to learn (article 28.1). Children seemed to view the purpose of school as twofold. For some hours in the morning and afternoon, it was a place where teachers set the rules but afterwards children were to take over the school building and define what to do themselves with other children only.

Children suggested improvement of the plan, therefore, was not in favor of including a teacher who decides everything on her own. They did not discuss decision making but instead described the perfect teacher as one who does not punish children every time they disobey the rules.

ES: A teacher who decides everything for you, prepares activities for you, tells you the rules and if you do not keep them, she will punish you.

I would not want [such a teacher].

ES: So what would you want the teacher to be like?

I would want one like the one we have now.

ES: What is your teacher like and you like her?

I do little silly things and she does not punish me every time.

ES: A teacher who is not strict! What else should a teacher do with children?

To be good.

ES: Anything else?

No.

The above comments indicated that article 12 was appreciated. The children referred back to the topics of rules about behavior in school and preferred a teacher who is not strict with discipline. Perhaps children felt that some teachers were harsh, thus, raising the significance of 28.2 of the Convention and articles 14(c) and 28 of GC 7 2005 about practices in school being child friendly and child centered.

Comparison of Children's Perspectives on the Social Environment

Children in Scotland wanted children to be consulted when the rules were set or any other decision was made as part of the improved plan for the best school ever. Furthermore, they talked about some of their ideas about aspects of life in school which they did not know how to impart to their teachers. Therefore, article 12 was important to them but they also needed article 5 to be fully or better implemented so that children can exercise their rights. Their views indicated that the large score in indulgence as well as the low score in power distance may have influenced them. Children did not want to be restrained without their consent and consultation for themselves and other children and they did not seem to accept their less powerful position.

In Greece, only children in Elm School agreed with the plan and with having the teacher set the rules. The rest of the groups wanted to be consulted and to have a say, which means that article 12 was important to them in terms of rule-making. Children in Pine School wanted to change their school rules, so that they can enjoy more time for play and more contact with other children. Children in Greece acknowledged their teachers as people who work in their best interests in terms of advocating for their requests (Elm School) or of knowing what children should do (Oak School).

However, only children from Elm School agreed with the idea of children co-deciding with their teachers about matters at school. Even though they were asked about decision making in general, children referred to rules rather than other matters. Children from Oak School wanted a teacher to tell children what the rules are but in a respectful way. Children from Pine School did not want a strict teacher when they break the rules.

To me, that means that children in Greece valued their teachers protecting them from harm and that they realized they need to learn how to be pupils or children in school, an institution or community new to them. I write new because children in Scotland were in primary school for the first time and preschool was not compulsory, whereas children in Greece were in kindergarten, the first year of compulsory education, too (even though it is not part of the primary school[13]). It could also be so due to the low score of individualism in Greece, which means more interference in children's life by adults. However, authors in Europe have also reported a tendency, in the Anglosphere, too, to teach children to depend on their teachers for conflict resolution (Alderson, 2008; Singer, 1996).

Part of this data, and not its analysis, was presented in my chapter entitled 'Young children's perceptions of a teacher-centred school: Voices from Scotland and Greece'. In S. M. Lange (2019), *Children's Rights: Global Perspectives, Challenges and Issues of the 21st Century* (pp. 33-57). Nova.

NOTES

[1] However, flora is not the only part of a natural environment. Fauna, sea, rivers, lakes, desserts, rocks, land, mountains, hills, clouds, winds, weather and climate are also included.

[2] This session took place in a part of their school library.

[3] They named two programs and, so, I used pseudonyms.

[4] The child who ran into the tree.

[5] For the teacher.

[6] Pointing to the corner of the table we were sitting at.

[7] A corner of play is a play area / center with a theme.

[8] Meaning a bench and tools.

[9] A pointer made by chenille stem.

[10] The boy was raising his hand.

[11] The teacher.

[12] Not all children in this group were classmates.

[13] At the time the focus group sessions took place, compulsory education in both countries began at age 5. However, in Greece children aged 5-6 were in kindergarten and not primary school, which means, for example, that officially they were not taught to the 3R's in the traditional way they are usually taught in primary. Nowadays in Greece, compulsory school begins at 4 years, again in kindergartens - the first type of school - followed by primary school (ages 6-12) and gymnasium /lower secondary (for ages 12-15).

CHAPTER 5

Children's Views About A School based on Developmental Psychology

Abstract: The data from the session in which children discussed the plan for a school based on developmental psychology are presented here. Children in both countries referred to aspects of provision and practice relating to children's right to education, play and participation. However, only children in Scotland talked about whether children should wear a uniform at school or not, raising the question of discrimination (article 2) and freedom of expression (article 13). Similarly, only children in Greece mentioned their fear for lack of protection from a hedge (article 19) around the schoolyard. When it comes to the social environment of the school, children in Scotland appreciated article 12 and children's right to be consulted and their views to be taken seriously according to their age and maturity a lot more than children in Greece.

Keywords: Developmental psychology, Non-discrimination, Right to play, Right to education, Right to participation, Right to safety.

INTRODUCTION

Children in both countries were read the following plan for the new school, which they were asked to improve.

In this school, the teacher and the children will decide together on many issues but not everything. The teacher will set some rules but she will also make some with the children. The teacher will prepare activities that she thinks children like. She will sometimes play with them in the corners and in the yard as if she were a little child herself. She will let children play a lot but she will want lessons, too. Around the school building, there will be a hedge. The yard will be large and some of it will be covered with grass and some of it with tartan. The yard will also have trees, a sand pit, a play house, monkey bars and a slide. Inside the school, there will be large rooms and a lot of stuff for the children such as toys, books, dolls, pastels, small tables and chairs and a clock. There will be no rows of desks or a big desk for the teacher.

Evanthia Synodi
All rights reserved-© 2023 Bentham Science Publishers

The Physical Environment of A School

Scotland

The groups of children who discussed a plan based on developmental psychology came from Valley primary school (a boy and two girls) and from Hill primary school (two boys and two girls) in Scotland. Children in both groups made comments on aspects of play for the improvement of the plan for a school for children of their age.

Valley School

Children from Valley School would add resources and equipment relevant to play, mostly sports, such as an obstacle course and a pool, to this plan for a school for young children. A garden with flowers, however, was their first suggestion. The inclusion of nature and the expansion of the size of the schoolyard to allow for movement and children being able to use their bodies were essential improvements to the yard.

Add flowers on it?

ES: You would add flowers. Ok. In the garden you mean?

Yeah.

Yeah.

Add obstacle courses[1]?

I like that idea.

ES: Ok. Any other ideas?

Trampoline.

A slide.

A swing.

ES: A slide? Oh, yes, I said it was going to have a slide, but I didn't say it was going to have a swing. Okay.

A swimming pool.

ES: Anything else?

Climbing frame.

ES: Climbing frame! Okay. Anything else?

A go cart.

A bike.

A two-wheel bike.

A two-wheel scooter.

We have loads of ideas.

Children did not mention any improvements for the indoors. It is as if the indoors was a place forbidden to them to question its perfection, perhaps because the plan was made by the queen and king's helpers. It is as if the school yard was the only place that interested them or that they had ideas about its improvement. This is on a par with Einarsdottir's (2005) findings. In her study children drew and photographed the outdoors as their most liked space. Perhaps the omission of the indoors in the discussion indicates a connection with Howard's (2010) and Wood's (2010) work on children distinguishing between play as the child's domain and work and learning as the teacher's domain and work. So, in classrooms, children learn / work and their teacher decides about their learning, whereas in the outdoors they play, which is their business. Article 31 on the children's right to play was prioritized. The implementation of article 29(e) regarding children learning respect for nature seems to be facilitated as children added flowers to the plan.

Hill School

Children in this group discussed the physical environment of the plan in relation to play, children's safety, their attire and their relaxation. They were concerned about fires at school and would add sprinklers and alarms and other ways of ensuring safety from fire in the school.

ES: So, do you think this school is fine? Would you suggest something else?

I think we should have like an art table.

ES: Art table? Would that be in the classroom or outside?

Um, in the classroom.

ES: In the classroom, okay.

Um, I think it would be much better, if in case there was a fire, there would be a slide, so if there was a fire, we would go down the giant slide.

ES: So, a fire slide.

Yeah.

Yes, and it would end at the sandpit.

If there was an electric fire and we would need, maybe we need help from the town.

I don't think we have a fire extinguisher.

ES: So, you think we should have fire extinguishers as well?

Yeah and also maybe some smoke alarms.

And sprinklers.

ES: And sprinklers?

The things on the top that pour all the water in case of fire.

How about we have some hoses on the walls? And they can shoot water if there is fire.

And buttons that start spraying water.

Why can't you make like a shower you can put outside? And then if there is a fire we can get the shower on and then it can spray water to get the fire out.

And if they get a fire slide for the bigger children, so that they won't hurt the little ones.

Article 19 and children's right to safety was a priority for the new plan. Then the children changed the subject and made suggestions about the appearance of the pupils in the new school, a topic not included in the plan. Some of them described a royal uniform and defended their idea saying that a uniform is a way of avoiding bullying, whereas others believed that children should be allowed to wear whatever they want at school.

ES: Anything else?

Have a playground where children can wear the same thing?

ES: What do you mean?

Maybe he means the children have on uniforms, not like shirts.

ES: Oh, right. So you don't want uniforms? Or you do?

No, we do. We want uniforms.

And maybe we could have like a badge for it. There should be a crown on it.

ES: A crown, okay, because it's a royal school, eh?

He nods yes.

Why can't we have a school where you can wear your own clothes to school? We don't need to wear uniforms.

ES: Okay, who thinks it's better if we don't wear uniforms?[2] Anna thinks so. Anyone else? Okay, the girls don't want uniforms and the boys want uniforms.

There was a clear gender split in their preference for pupils' attire in school. The boys seemed to value the right children have not to be discriminated against for their clothes (article 2), which bullies do not respect, so they advocated uniforms. The girls valued the children's right to have freedom of expression (article 13) in terms of what to wear and article 2, children's right not to be discriminated against by anybody in school, including bullies.

The debate about the attire in school continued. The girls showed a willingness to compromise their idea of wearing whatever they want to school but the boys did not change their minds about wearing uniforms at school.

I think I have got an idea. How about two of the days we have uniforms on and the rest of the days we have no uniforms?

ES: What do you think, boys?

I think they should have uniform every day. Um, because they, um, people might tease people about their clothes and things like that.

Why can't people just wear whatever they want to school?

Because it's a royal school. So they can still have a sawn badge on it. So they can still have the badge of the crown on it.

ES: So, if it wasn't a royal school, would it matter if they wore uniforms?

Yeah, because sometimes at royal school ...

They wear smart clothes.

No, but we all wear smart clothes, school uniforms are smart clothes.

Not like a pretty princess dress.

No, no.

Children could not reach an agreement as a group. Article 2 (non discrimination) was important to all of them but for the two girls of the group, it was combined with article 13 (right to free expression).

These children also made suggestions about play equipment and resources as well as the location and size of the new school. They wanted flora in the yard, a maze and a waterpark with all other resources children need to enjoy playing there. Ice cream was essential and for the plan of this royal school, the boys wanted the queen and king to buy ice cream makers.

How about we have a little maze in the garden?

Oh!

Oh, yes!

Yeah!

ES: A maze in the garden.

So they can play like cricket in the school.

ES: So, in this school we should have a big garden with a maze. Okay. Anything else you would like a school to have to be the best school ever?

A big green house with flowers and strawberries and fruit which they can have by the school, that's nice.

Oh, yeah, that would be a good idea.

A massive waterpark.

ES: A massive waterpark?

Yeah.

Yeah.

In the summer, we can play in the water.

If it is sunny.

And school wet suits [swimming suits] and we can have water fights.

And have water pistols for each class.

I think we should build a castle at the sea, near the seaside so if they are really, really good, the class can go on a trip to the seaside and they can have a shot at swimming in the sea.

ES: So you want to build a castle by the seaside?

Yeah, so like, it's near the seaside and close to the school.

ES: Oh so you want a school close to the sea?

Yeah.

Like (the sea is) across the road (from the school).

I want it to be, like, ginormous.

ES: Big one?

Yeah.

And ten times the size of the school we've got.

And ten times better than this school.

And a garden.

A giant ice cream van that sells every kind of ice cream.

Or they could get ice-cream makers in the class, cause it's a royal school.

Most of the children's suggestions were about the yard and included a maze, a waterpark and a garden. These children indicated that the school of the plan should be larger. The expression they used was 'ten times the size of the school we've got'. This means that article 31 on play and leisure was important to them. Children mentioned flowers, fruit, the sea and seaside as important to the new school, which shows that article 29(e) on education developing respect for the natural environment in children at school has a strong basis for success.

Being compensated for being 'really, really good' was expected by children, as their suggestions for reward (*i.e.* going to the seaside or having ice-cream) show. This finding on rewards for following the school rules is similar to the star time, *i.e.* time for children to play as a reward in school discussed by Sirkko, Kyronlampi and Puroila (2019). It is a behavioristic technique employed in teacher-centered schools (as discussed in Chapter 2).

Greece

Three groups from three kindergartens in Greece discussed the physical environment of the plan for a school based on developmental psychology. Their answers were relevant to play, particularly in the yard, as well as to children's safety. The group from Elm School was made up of boys only; the rest of the groups included both boys and girls.

Elm School

Children in this group did not have much to add to the physical environment of the school I had described to them. Their only new suggestion was that it had flowers. They also elaborated on the trees of the schoolyard, which were to include palm trees and fruit trees.

ES: I want you to tell me if you like the plan or not.

I like it.

I like it, too.

Me too.

ES: What do you like about it?

Everything.

I like everything, too.

Me, too.

ES: Can you tell me one of these many things?

Yes.

Sand.

Flowers, trees, palm trees.

Maybe also trees that make fruit.

Nature, in the form of flowers, palm trees and fruit trees in school was important for this group. Their answers indicated the scope for the successful implementation of article 29(e).

Oak School

Children in the Oak School gave a lot of suggestions to make the physical environment of the plan for a school better. The boys in this group expressed reservations about the protection a hedge could offer in comparison to a low cement wall around the school wall. Boys were concerned with the implementation of article 19 and children's right to safety. The girls liked the idea of bushes around the schoolyard but did not justify their view.

ES: Let me tell you how the schoolyard would have been like. They would put trees and bushes all around it.

No.

ES: Why not?

Because if there is no wire netting, the plants may fall down and break.

Cement to place the wire netting on is stronger than trees.

I agree.

ES: You girls, what do you say? Wires or plants? Which one would you like the most?

Plants.

When discussing the contents of the schoolyard, this group would add more equipment for play. Some of their suggestions, such as a pond, a pool or keeping a horse and other animals, would require an even larger yard, but they did not talk about it.

ES: The yard will be large and some of it will be covered with grass and some of it with tartan. The yard will also have trees, a sand pit, a play house, a climber and a slide. How do you feel about such a yard?

Perfect! I wish we had it!

ES: Would you place anything else?

Yes, a trampoline.

A big inflatable toy.

Pool.

ES: What else?

Slides, water slides.

A bicycle.

I want a bicycle, too.

A bee hive to make honey.

A pond.

ES: Just a pond?

Little ducks.

And hens so as to eat eggs.

An apple tree.

Butterflies.

I do not like butterflies.

Dogs to take care of.

A horse.

ES: Any other idea for the yard?

A ball to play football.

And one (ball) to play volleyball.

Treasure hunt.

Children in this group linked the yard with play (article 31) and with nature (article 29(e)). In the yard, children can play and get in touch with animals and flora, which is a good start for the implementation of article 29(e) about children's right to an education teaching them to respect the natural environment.

These children also discussed the indoors of the school, unlike children in Elm School. They would add a clown, balloons, legos, toy spiders, toy shovels, computers, tablets and toy trucks in the classrooms.

ES: Inside the school, there will be large rooms and a lot of stuff for the children such as toys, books, dolls, pastels, small tables and chairs and a clock. There will be no rows of desks or a big desk for the teacher.

And a clown to make funny things for us.

ES: What else should the classroom have?

Balloons.

(Toy) Spiders so that each one of us can become spider-man.

Legos.

ES: Anything else to have in the classroom?

A bone for the dog.

ES: Will you keep it (the bone) in the classroom?

Yes, to throw it like this.

We will be shepherds.

(Toy) shovels.

Coloring markers.

To have a bed.v

ES: Indoors?

In the yard.

And little birds.

Painting.

ES: Anything else?

A computer.

A mobile.

A tablet.

Lady bugs.

Toy trucks.

Books.

Toy motorcycles.

What these children would add to a classroom is related to play and the arts. Their love for animals was so strong that (a) one of them realized that it would make them *shepherds* and (b) that they even added little birds and ladybugs to the yard, while discussing the indoors. Furthermore, technology (*e.g.* computers, tablets, which were not included in the plan) and books (which were included in the plan) were mentioned. These resources could be used in activities initiated both by teachers and by children. So, this group extended play and child-initiated activities in the classroom, even though some of the resources they mentioned did not exclude activities directed by their teacher. Article 28.1 on children's right to education was reflected in their views as well as article 31 and children right to play, rest and leisure, as the children would like the new school to have a bed for them to lie in in the yard.

Pine School

These children's suggestions were influenced by the classroom organization of the Greek kindergarten, which has areas or corners. Children included items relevant to teaching children, like boards, circle time, worksheets and projectors. Furthermore, they described aspects of being a pupil, such as 'doing work', 'cleaning' and 'tidying up' in the classroom. None of the other groups who were read this plan made connections between the physical environment of the new school, rules and learning to be a pupil.

Won't they have a carpet for circle time?

ES: Oh, to add a circle time carpet? Okay. Is this plan perfect or are there things missing?

To do work, because if they play all the time they will not learn to read and write.

This child thought that, and the others in the groups did not disagree, children in this new school would only play or mainly play, even though the plan was for both play and lessons.

ES: Do you mean the teacher should give them worksheets[3]?

Yes.

ES: And what else should there be in the classroom?

A board. They can also tell the months, the days and other things we do.

ES: Anything else?

And teachers to have the children clean the whole school.

And teachers to take lunch [with them to school] and have it with them (the children).

ES: Do you mean [bring lunch] from home[4]?

Yes.

ES: What else should the classroom have to be perfect?

I know, let's put some corners.

And a big television.

Let them put in a projector as well.

ES: And what corners should it have?

Kitchen and shelves and a bookcase and shelves with tools.

Board games and puzzles and legos and dice.

ES: What else?

Loud speakers.

Children should put their toys back in their place.

(Children) should keep the tables clean and not dirty them.

These children clearly linked learning to the physical environment of the classroom, which did not exclude play (board games, legos, *etc.*). However, it is clear from their suggestions that the classroom is a space where children learn (a) what they are taught as well as (b) how to be pupils. What children should be taught in the new school was what was available in their own school. It had to do with the 3R's as well as other extensions given to the 3 R's, such as working, cleaning, and tidying up (Morgan & Robinson, 1976), which I refer to as being a pupil. Their answers reflect a combination of articles 31 and children right to play, 28.1 and children right to education and 29(a) and children right to an education that develops their mental abilities.

As for the outdoors, they would add play equipment, flowers, snails, chairs, bonfires and railings around the yard. Then children started to discuss the indoors again. They added improvements on the building, which were: a storage place, furniture for the children's stuff and a desk for the teacher, which was to be placed either in the classroom or in a separate office.

ES: What about the perfect yard?

Swings.

To have two, at least two (swings), so that all children can fit (meaning that they would not have to wait long).

ES: What else should they have in their yard?

Chairs.

A bond fire.

Not to have accidents.

To have flowers behind the stone partings, like the ones we have.

ES: Ah, flowers, too! Anything else?

To have a storage place in the school building.

And snails.

And a desk.

Hangers.

ES: Who will the desk be for?

For the teacher.

ES: Where will the teacher's desk be, in the classroom or in another room?

In another room, because in the classroom children will not let her concentrate.

No.

ES: And you, Helen⁵, what do you think? Should the teacher's desk to be in the classroom?

Yes, so that she can keep an eye on the children because they are naughty when the teacher leaves the room.

To have shelves outside their classroom door (for the children) to place their bags and to have bars and railings put outside (not hedges).

To have folders (to put their worksheets or drawings).

Provision for children's safety (article 19) was important for this group not only in terms of the physical boundaries around the yard but also in not having accidents in it, with the fires lit and chairs left in the yard. Therefore, articles 19 and 31 (rest and leisure) were important to them. Nature (*e.g.* flowers, snails) was also necessary for a perfect school, so the implementation of article 29(e) would at the same time be facilitated in the new school.

Children had two different views on where the teacher's desk should be placed, even though the plan clarified that a teacher's desk would not be in the classroom. One child explained that teachers were to stop them from being naughty so their desks should be in the classroom but another argued that teachers are not able to concentrate at their desks with so many children around. So, they believed that children make a lot of noise or mischiefs and this makes the teachers' presence around them all the time necessary.

Children described themselves as naughty rather than some behaviors children may exhibit in the way other children in this study said, for example, that they make '*silly little things*'. Children thinking of other children as naughty points to the model of the evil child who has to be taught how to behave, who needs somebody to keep an eye on them, which has been internalized by some children. Eisarsdottir (2005) found a similar tendency in her study. Some girls discussed discipline in school 'with the eyes of an outsider' (Eisarsdottir, 2005, p. 477) when talking about other children not being able to learn the rules in the same way girls in the group from Pine School called other children naughty.

Comparison of Children's Perspectives on the Physical Environment

Most of the resources children mentioned were relevant to play, relaxation and contact with nature in school (trampolines, pools, animals, fruit trees, flowers) outdoors (both countries) and to a lesser extent indoors. Only three of the five groups in both countries talked about the classroom environment (in Oak School [*e.g.* tablets, computers] and Pine School [*e.g.* markers, legos] in Greece and one mention in Hill School [art table] in Scotland). Therefore, article 31 on children's right to play was a priority in both countries.

Children in Hill School in Scotland and in Oak and Pine kindergartens in Greece expressed concerns about different issues of safety at school. Children in Scotland were concerned about fires in school, which was not included in the plan, whereas children in Greece were concerned about the protection that a hedge around the school could not offer them, which was included in the plan. Some children in Oak School and Pine School did not want a hedge around the schoolyard. So, for different reasons article 19 was important to most children in both countries.

Their improvements to the plan for a school also included references to children's attire in Scotland (Hill School) and to learning in Greece (Oak School and Pine School). Some children in Hill School in Scotland mentioned school uniforms as a necessary addition to the plan whereas children in Greece mentioned books and tablets (Oak School) and circle time and worksheets (Pine School) as missing from the classroom described to them. However, resources such as tablets and computers can be used by children in their own activities, which means a combination of articles 28.1 and 31. Children from Pine School referred to teaching (*i.e.* circle time) so article 28.1 was important to them.

However, pupils wearing uniforms (Hill School) and completing worksheets (Pine School) are aspects of a teacher-centered school, which does not respect or acknowledge children's rights. Girls in Hill School and in Oak School held different views compared to the boys in their respective groups. In Hill School, girls did not want to wear uniforms to school and their justification prioritized articles 2 and 13. Girls in Oak School wanted hedges around the school rather than wire netting, even though they could not justify their answer.

Social Environment of A School

Scotland

Both groups of children in Scotland discussed the processes of rule-setting and decision-making described in the plan for a school based on developmental psychology. Children wanted to be consulted on both occasions.

Valley School

Children thought it important for the teacher to make some rules so that children know what is expected of them but also for children to make some, because children may have a rule to suggest. They believed that children could have some input into school life in terms of rule-making.

ES: You know the plan is for the teacher to make some rules herself, and some other rules with the children. Do you think it's a good idea?

I think it's a good idea.

Me too.

Uh huh.

ES: Why?

Because the children might know what she is talking about?

The children may have a very good idea.

Their views are in accordance with article 12 as well as article 33 of GC 2005. The Comment explains that human rights education is to be provided in school in the form of opportunities for children to practice their rights in accordance with their interests, concerns and capabilities.

These children did not talk about the idea of children in the new school making some decisions with their teachers. However, they discussed the possibility of themselves talking to their teachers about co-deciding on school matters.

ES: So, how do you feel about sharing some of the decisions with your teacher?

Good.

I feel fine.

I feel excellent doing that.

ES: So, what decision would you like to make with your teacher? Can you think of something?

I don't know.

Me neither.

ES: I'm talking about things that you can do in school. I'm talking about decisions, like, perhaps you want to do less writing or less maths?

I want to do longer, longer, longer, longer writing.

ES: You want more writing? Okay.

I want to make more homework.

ES: You want more homework.

Me too.

Me too.

ES: Alright. Do you ever tell your teacher about that?

No.

ES: Why not?

I just don't think what decision to do.

Me, too.

ES: Oh, right. So, you thought about it today for the first time?

Yeah.

The implementation of article 12 was welcome but children did not seem to know how to fulfill it. Therefore, action needs to be taken in relation to the implementation of article 5, which foresees children's right to guidance and direction from adults in learning and exercising their rights. Children's right to education (articles 28.1 and 29(a)) was also linked to sharing decisions with their teachers, as children wanted to go to school and do reading, writing, mathematics and have homework. This group has accepted some aspects of what traditionally takes place in a primary school (curriculum and practices), but they also wanted to play more, which their primary education did not allow.

Hill School

Children in this group did not talk about the way of setting the rules in the new school. Instead they talked about the rules that children must follow in the school the queen and the king planned. They suggested the new school adopted the rules they had in their school. Therefore, being gentle and honest, not fighting with others and pacing oneself while moving were the rules which should govern aspects of child relationships with other people in the new school. Children also recommended the same treatment of disobedience as they had in their own school, which was being taken to the head teacher to decide the repercussions of disobedience.

Maybe they can copy our Hill School[6] rules? I can't even remember any of the Hill School rules.

Maybe being gentle.

And being honest.

What about not running in the classroom?

Only walking (in the classroom), only running outside.

ES: Okay only running outside. Anything else?

No fighting.

No fighting or they go straight to the head teacher.

ES: No fighting, okay. Alright. And if somebody doesn't follow the rules, who should decide their punishment?

I think it should be ... the head teacher.

The teacher.

ES: Wouldn't you want to have a say?

I think it should be ... decide like, the teachers. Like outside cause we don't have teachers outside[7] and if they're fighting outside we've got to tell the teacher, they decide to tell the head teacher.

ES: Okay. So you want the adults, the grown-ups to decide.

Yeah.

And then if they go to the head teacher, they just give them a big growl!

These children suggested to the queen and king that they adopt their rules for their new school. The rules in Hill School mentioned by the children indicated the importance of article 19 on children right to physical safety. Children emphasized their teacher's role in protecting them from other children harming them (*e.g.* when fighting), which was the most important rule. At the same time, they could not even imagine that how to treat those who break a rule is a topic that concerns classmates as well as the child who misbehaved and the adults. They did not consider treating misbehavior as a decision affecting their lives in the making of which they should be consulted (article 12).

Children in this school liked the idea of children co-deciding some things with their teachers every day and claimed that they do so with their teachers. They also suggested children in the new school have star[8] time, like they did. The discussion that followed focused on issues they wanted to decide with their teacher, such as what to eat and changing the location of the girls' bathroom in relation to the dinner hall, because it was too far away, whereas the boys' were very close.

ES: Well, they are planning to decide some things together, the children and the teacher, they will decide some things together, but not everything. How do you feel about that?

I feel that to decide like, um, the teacher and children decide like, one thing a day, and also the teacher to decide one thing.

ES: Okay, can you give us an example? What is the one thing you think the teacher should decide a day? And one of the other things.

I think they should decide which time ... um they are going to do things.

ES: Okay, so their daily routine you mean. When they are going to do and what. And what should the children decide? You'll talk, girls, just let him finish.

Um, but the children and the teacher always decide everything else.

Like what?

How about they have a star time?

ES: Everyday?

No.

No.

Only on Fridays too, because we have got it on Fridays.

ES: So, this school also should have star time.

On Fridays, too.

ES: On Fridays. So it'll be star time on Friday.

Why can't at lunch time people can have a toilet in the middle of their lunch hall so they can leave their trays only if they need the toilet. Because we have to go ...

Go all the way round ...

If we want to, we have to go to like straight on and then down the stairs.

ES: So, you're saying you would like the toilets to be next to the lunch hall.

Because the girls are really bursting, they have to go really far to the girls' toilets.

As Jack did not had a chance to answer what children should decide I asked:

ES: Okay. So what about decisions and choices? Jack said the teacher should decide the time of the activities, but the rest she should decide with the children.

Yeah.

ES: Can you give me an example? What things would you like them to decide with the teacher? What things?

Maybe they could decide that they don't have the dinner chips.

ES: So, children should decide about their food.

Yeah, you can have packed lunches and school dinners, because that's what we do here.

Yeah, that's what we do.

Yeah, we choose our own dinners.

Yeah!

ES: *Choose your own dinner, you mean what you are going to eat?*

Yeah.

ES: *Not if it is packed or not but what exactly you are going to eat. Like if it is rice or potatoes or something like that?*

Yeah.

A little later, I asked them:

ES: *How do you feel about making decisions with your teacher?*

Quite good.

Good.

Everyone says 'yeah'.

ES: *Does this mean you make decisions with your teacher?*

Yeah. Sometimes.

ES: *Sometimes? Can you give me an example? Was there a time you made a decision with your teacher?*

She asked me if I wanted to have a little show of basketball and I said yes.

Children liked the idea of children sharing decision-making with their teachers about some things. Children related decision-making to their immediate experiences in school and in particular to eating and playing arrangements. They recommended that in the new school children decide about these two arrangements and they seemed to appreciate the chance to do so. Article 12 was appreciated by these children and they also had topics to raise with their teachers. Somehow their answers indicated that they did not talk to their teachers about their problems, such as food and bathroom location. Article 5 needs to be further related to education and teachers' tasks in order for the implementation of article 12 to be facilitated.

Greece

In Greece, only one group commented on the issue of children setting rules and making decisions with their teachers in the new school. They wanted to be consulted about setting rules but they wanted their teacher to make decisions.

Oak School

This group believed that children should make some rules with their teachers. However, the only rule they could think of was about playing football in the yard. Their yard was proportionately small for so many children and their teachers would not let them play football whenever the children wanted to.

ES: You know the plan is for the teacher to make some rules herself, and some other rules with the children. How do you feel about that?

Good idea!

If your teacher let you make a rule, what rule would you make?

Not to hit others.

ES: Isn't this a rule in your school already?

Yes, it is.

ES: Which new rule would you make?

Not to hit others.

Not to make fun of others.

To play football.

ES: Where would you play football?

In the yard.

Just like children from Hill School, these children could not think of rules different from the ones they had in their school. This may be so, because children never had the opportunity to be consulted about rule-making in school. Perhaps they have not been given the opportunity to develop skills enabling them to exercise their right as defined by article 12 of the Convention. This raises the need to extend the implementation of article 5 in schools further.

Although rules about protecting and respecting children dignity (*i.e.* not making fun of others) and safety rules (not hitting others) were raised, children had not linked rules to the teachers' intention of protecting them from possible harm (article 19) from playing football in a small yard. Their answers indicate that their rights to play (article 31), to safety (article 19) and to dignity (Preamble of the Convention and article 28.2) were important to all of them. Sharing, however, rule-making was welcome and appreciated, even though they did not expand on it. So article 12 as further explained in article 33 of GC 2005 was important to them.

Children from Oak School believed that the teacher should decide and not the children because decisions are for grown-ups who know what should be done.

ES: Who will decide?

The teacher.

I say the teacher, too.

Why the teacher?

Because the teacher is a grown-up and knows.

A possible interpretation of this dialog is that children believed in different jurisdictions and roles for children and adults in school, which, in a sense is correct. However, it is strange that these children could not think of expressing any dislikes they may have for how things were done by teachers in their school or for whatever took place in their school. Such a reply is relevant to the degree of individualism in Greece which is low and almost one-third of what it is in Scotland (35 as compared to 91 for UK). As already stated, a low score in individualism means that children become members of strong groups, which protect them and to which children owe loyalty (Farlane, 2018; Hofstede, 2021b). The degree to which schools in countries with low individualism teach children 'to be independent, to think and act for' themselves, 'to make' their 'own decisions' (Farlane, 2018, p. 133) is low. This explains why article 12 was not even hinted at this point. It also indicates the importance of better provision for the implementation of article 5, which foresees that children must be provided with guidance and direction when they cannot yet exercise their rights.

Comparison of Children's Perspectives on the Social Environment

Children from the groups from Valley School in Scotland and from Oak School in Greece were in favor of children making some rules with their teachers, as the plan read to them said. However, only children from Valley School saw a purpose in sharing rule-making, which was that children know what their teachers talk about and that children ideas may be put to use. Children from Oak School did not explain their views, but suggested the adoption of rules of their own school as an improvement to the plan they were read. Children from Hill School did not discuss rule making at all, but thought that children in the new school should follow the rules of Hill School and that teachers are the protectors of children's safety when punishing those who break rules.

Regarding who should make decisions in school, both groups in Scotland said they would like children as well as themselves to decide things with their teachers whereas children from Oak School in Greece believed that teachers should make decisions in school. Therefore, children in Scotland prioritized article 12 but children in Oak School did not consider themselves capable of sharing decision-making. This indicates that a lot more action needs to be taken for the implementation of article 5 in Greece.

NOTES

[1] I think the mention of tartan made children in Scotland think of obstacle courses but that was not so in Greece.

[2] The children did not speak, they raised their hands.

[3] Worksheets was the first thing that came to my mind as an example of work and I told the children so as to make them clarify work some more. The official curriculum for kindergarten rejects worksheets but a number of teachers saw them as worthwhile and used them.

[4] In Greece, some children could stay at kindergarten for the afternoon session as well. The morning session was available and compulsory to all five year olds at the time of the focus group sessions. Children who stayed for both school sessions brought their lunches in containers which were kept in the school refrigerator and were heated by their teachers at lunch time. None of the three participating kindergartens had dinner halls or dinner ladies.

⁵ She raised her hand.

⁶ I used the name of Hill school to replace their term for reasons of anonymity.

⁷ In this particular school, school assistants were in the yard during breaks.

⁸ I have borrowed the term *star time* from Sirkko, Kyronlampi, and Puroila (2019) to provide for anonymity. The concept behind this star time was the same as in Hill school; it was play time and resources mainly used to reward children every Friday.

CHAPTER 6

Children's Views About A Rights-based School

Abstract: Children discussed the plan for a school respecting and implementing all of their rights and their views are analyzed here. They added more resources to their physical environment which were relevant to their right to play mainly and this tendency was stronger in Greece as compared to Scotland. In terms of suggestions for a school for young children, these were influenced by the provision of education children received in their countries respectively. As for the social environment, children in both countries showed an appreciation of article 12 and wanted to participate in decision-making, even though they did not know which decisions or how. This need raised the importance of article 5 and the importance of adults helping children exercise their rights.

Keywords: Indulgence, Individualism, Right to play, Right to education, Right to safety, Rights-based school.

INTRODUCTION

Only children from Valley School in Scotland were read the following plan for a rights-based school and were asked to discuss it because there were not enough participants from Hill School. However, there were three groups, one from each of the participating schools in Greece.

In this school the children and the teachers will decide together about all the school problems. They will decide what they will do with children and teachers who do not treat others well or if they go visit a museum. In this school the children and the teachers will decide all of the rules together. The teacher will ask the children what they want to do and learn and that is what they will do. Children will play everywhere in the school; in the corners, in the gym, in the yard and in the forest with their teachers and with other children. Their teachers will never interrupt their play to start other activities. They will not put wire or bushes around the yard. The school yard will have grass but also tartan. There will also be trees, a sand pit, a play house, a jungle gym, a seesaw, a climber and a slide. The school will have large and tiny rooms. They will put a lot of stuff inside for the children such as toys, books, teddy bears, crayons, tricycles, dough, furniture,

Evanthia Synodi
All rights reserved-© 2023 Bentham Science Publishers

big and small, cement, plaster, wood, thermometers, tubes, scissors, spatulas, knives and saws.

The Physical Environment of the School

Scotland

There was only one group of children from Valley School in the sample from Scotland who discussed the plan for a rights-based school. They were concerned with learning resources and practices and barely talked about the play.

Valley School

When asked the first general question about how to make the rights-based school described to them perfect, children included very few play resources *i.e.* balls and obstacle courses. Tartan was linked to an obstacle course and was not perceived as a safe floor for play outdoors, as it was intended by the plan. They focused on children learning, on teaching, which was broadly defined in one sentence in the plan[1] , and on time spent on the play. They believed that children in this school should spend more time learning rather than playing, even though the plan did not say how much time children would spend on work / learning and play / child led activities in school. Children referred to the part school plays in developing children physical skills, social skills, and life attitudes. More particularly, they talked about learning more mathematics, doing more writing and worksheets, learning about money and paying bills, becoming able not to spill food and drinks, doing gymnastics, not hurting others and not giving up when they fail. These children seemed to have identified the materials and equipment of the plan as play-related, even though, traditionally, real thermometers, knives, saws and tubes, for instance, are not allowed to be used as play resources in schools.

We could put some more things in the playground and stuff, you know, so, many balls and we could have some other things into the obstacle course?

They need to do more learning.

ES: More learning. Ok, Like what?

Like, how to count up.

ES: Anything else they should be learning?

How to count down.

ES: Count up and down. Ok.

Maybe we could learn more things to do with maths.

Maybe not play so much?

ES: Alright. Not play so much. Why do you think they shouldn't play that much?

Because they won't know anything when somebody asks them a question.

ES: Alright. They will not know anything if somebody asks them questions. And is that more important than playing?

Christine nods yes.

ES: You think so? Ok.

They might want to learn not to kick the ball in their face because somebody might get hurt and fall over.

ES: Anything else to make it the best school ever? Any other ideas that these children may have forgotten?

Maybe we could ... we could maybe learn the time properly?

Maybe they should learn about money a bit more, cause they may not know what money is.

ES: Ok. Learning about money. Yes.

Em ... they may have to learn how to pay.

And get food and drink not spilled.

ES: Oh, they need to learn to pay what?

Pay and buy and see if they have enough money to buy food and drinks.

They could have some worksheets and blue folders?

ES: Worksheets and blue folders. So, what exactly do you do with the blue folders? I don't know.

You put your...you put your work in it.

ES: Alright. In the folder. Is that what you wanted to say?

No (he wanted to say something else), but ... yeah (we use folders in our school). We are usually given books, which we have in our school bags and they may have trays to put stuff in.

ES: *Oh, trays. So you think that is a good idea for the new school as well? Ok. Anything else?*

Maybe we could work more.

ES: *Ok. Like Christine said, not play so much. You're saying to work more.*

Yeah.

ES: *What kind of work? What do you mean when you say work more?*

We could maybe have a worksheet that you can circle, circle some things that you know.

ES: *Alright.*

They may have some postcards in case people are sick and they can't go to school and then they can send stuff and draw things on.

Uh huh.

And also learn how to draw and write.

ES: *Learn to draw and write. Ok. Anything else?*

Learn not to fall off and try again?

ES: *Right. So, to learn not to fall and if you fall, try again.*

(Mick nods yes).

To learn how to do ... Neat writing. When you have a pencil and you try to do neat writing.

ES: *Yes. Anything else?*

Maybe they could do gym.

ES: *Gym as well? Ok.*

And learn to do some gymnastics and handstand or headstands.

For this group of children, what young children learn at school was not defined in terms broader than what they perceived (or even experienced) learning to be in primary school. Learning had to do with the 3R's and their application to children lives, then and later. They were not to play 'so much'. To these children, children's right to education in terms of articles 28.1 and 29(a) was a priority and to a lesser extent children's right to play (article 31). They thought that children needed to learn these things so as to be able to answer questions asked. To me, this is an idea cultivated by adults. I have been hearing about it ever since I was a child myself; it was supposed to be a motivator for children to become pupils quietly and peacefully. This view is in accordance with the philosophy of an authoritarian school, where children learn what adults think that children will need in the future (see Chapter 2).

Greece

Children from Greece suggested more materials for play at school and a different classroom and yard organization based on the layout of their own school. Children from two out of the three kindergartens in the Greek sample expressed concerns about children's safety while in school caused by the physical environment as described in the plan.

Elm School

Children welcomed the idea of children using real tools, such as knives and saws. They did not offer any new suggestions on resources or facilities, except for plasticine.

ES: The school will have large and tiny rooms. They will put a lot of stuff inside for the children such as toys, books, teddy bears, crayons, tricycles, dough, furniture, big and small, cement, plaster, wood, thermometers, tubes, scissors, spatulas, knives and saws.

So good that the children know how to use knives!

The teacher will show them how.

Are they toys (toy knives)?

ES: No, they will have real ones in order to learn how to use them.

And when they grow up they will know and will not get cut.

And saws?

ES: Both the saws and the knives (will be real).

A little later, I asked:

ES: Good. Did you like the indoors?

Yes.

Yes, I liked it a little.

Yes.

ES: What did you like about it?

That it would have a gym and plasticines.

This group was also concerned about children safety since there would not be a fence or hedge around the school. However, one of these children also made a small comment on how they liked children co-deciding with the queen and king, which nobody else from any of the other groups from both countries did.

ES: Can you tell me what you liked most about the plan for a kindergarten that I read to you?

I liked the playhouse.

I liked the king and queen.

ES: What do you mean?

When they decided with the children.

I was a little surprised because they did not put railings. Maybe somebody will go and leave garbage there and the children may slip and fall and get seriously hurt!

ES: But have you considered that the yard would be very large and the children will be able to run and to play wherever they want?

Yes, but they may get lost.

Maybe the teachers can go look for them or some children who know it very well.

They'd better go on excursions with their teachers.

I did not like this kindergarten much because if there are no railings, children can go far and get lost and their moms and dads will cry. They may not know the way back and they will be crying.

The only things I did not like it that there are no railings.

Me, too.

Me, too.

Maybe the teacher and we, the children, did not see a child and somebody bad goes there and throws the child down and they hurt them seriously.

According to children, teachers at school should show children how to use tools and prevent them from getting lost or harmed. Protection from physical harm (article 19), therefore, was important to these children and formed part of the teachers' job description. I think that here children expressed fear which has been inculcated in them by adults. This group was afraid that children would get lost because their schoolyard would be large, even though their fear and concern were for the feelings of people other than the children themselves. This group was also afraid (a) for children slipping on the garbage, as if their school was built next to a landfill or in a place without dumpsters or dustbins and (b) of bad people who can throw children down and hurt them. However, the school these children attended was in a safe and clean area, which reinforces my understanding that fear for all these factors was the adults' fears, which seeped into children's minds.

Children's rights to education (articles 28.1 and 29(a)) and to play (article 31) were also appreciated, as this group mentioned developing their physical abilities using tools, the gym, and plasticine.

Oak School

These children had more materials to add to the plan for a perfect school, such as paintbrushes, markers, notebooks, books, and computers. Books were included in the original plan but they repeated them. Swings, blackboards, benches, tables and a circle time area were added to the plan, which were equipment and facilities they had in their own kindergarten. They were the only group in the Greek sample who did not reject the idea of no fences, railings or hedges, together with the group from Valley School.

ES: ... All these so that the children can make stuff and play.

I like it.

We want all of these.

ES: Would you like it to have anything else besides these stuff the children said?

Yes.

Paint brushes.

Markers, notebooks.

Computers.

Benches.

Little bugs.

Tables.

Puzzles.

To have a balcony and furniture with drawers.

ES: One last thing, in the yard they do not want it to have wire all around it.

What?

ES: All this thing around the yard where the door locks, they do not want to have that at all at school.

Not even a lock?

Because they want to go through freely and get out freely?

ES: Yes, for that. And they also want the yard to have trees and sand and tartan so that the children do not get hurt when they play, to have a play house, seesaws, jungle bars and slides. What do you think about such a yard?

I like this yard very much.

ES: *Michael do you like this yard? Would you like it to have something else as well?*

No.

I want it to have a swing.

ES: *Right, to have swings as well.*

Books.

ES: *Books in the yard?*

No, inside.

And a blackboard.

I know! A circle place to sit in.

The most important article for these children was article 31, which refers to children's right to play. Article 28.1 about their right to education was important, too, as they mentioned features related to teaching, such as a board and circle time.

Pine School

Children in this school suggested toy knives instead of real ones and added toy bombs, toys guns and toy weapons. No risks to physical safety that real knives and saws entail were acceptable, even though their use leads to the development of children's motor skills. They suggested more play resources for the school; a hospital area, a pastry shop area, a baby-doll area and a play station.

ES: *Children have asked for all these things. How do you feel about it?*

They need gauze and injections because I want to make a corner for the children to play doctor and have dolls, those special ones [gauzes] for the hospital.

ES: *So, to add gauzes and syringes so that they can play in the doctor's corner, you say.*

Ma'am, can I tell you something? A friend of mine has a doll that wears a band aid and when she pulls it, it (the wound) is red. And it has many things and a lotion and when you put it on, the redness goes away. The wound becomes smaller and so you put the band aid on and then the redness appears again and all over again. It has band aids, a feeding bottle, nappies and other stuff.

ES: *So, to have such a doll at the kindergarten?*

Yes.

A PlayStation.

ES: *Let me tell you another thing. The children do not want a wire fence or a hedge around the yard and they want the yard to have trees, sand, tartan so as not to get hurt when they fall.*

Where we have the hopscotch [drawn on the playground in Pine School] there is no soft material and we may fall and open a big wound.

ES: *So, in the hopscotch area to have soft material?*

Yes, and it should also have other games with numbers [painted on the ground outdoors].

ES: *The children also asked for a playhouse, seesaw, jungle bars and slides.*

We do not have jungle bars.

ES: *Do you like the idea of having jungle bars?*

Yes.

A corner that has baby-dolls and other stuff to take care of the babies [baby-dolls] in the yard and in the classroom.

ES: *You, boys, have not said anything. Do you like their ideas? Have you got anything else to suggest?*

Nick: *We want weapons, knives, guns, bombs ...*

Toys, not real ones.

ES: *You, Bert, what do you say? Would you like the kindergarten to have anything else?*

I want a pastry shop corner with toy sweets and other stuff from the pastry shop, toy pastry shop, and a little house that has the label pastry shop on it.

ES: To have it indoors, right?

And take it outdoors.

All of the children suggestions for the improvement of the plan had to do with the further implementation of article 31 and children's right to play.

Comparison of Children's Views on the Physical Environment

Based on the plan of the rights-based school, children in Scotland made very few comments on the physical environment. Children from all three schools in Greece made more, even though this plan included the richest description of the play and learning environment indoors and outdoors in comparison with the other two I wrote. Children from Valley School as well as children from Pine School did not discuss the lack of physical boundaries in the yard, whereas children from Elm and Oak Schools in Greece did. None of the groups in Greece made any comments relevant to space and time dedicated to play and child-initiated activities. However, children in Valley School thought the time dedicated to play was too much, because they misinterpreted the plan. The plan was that children play will not be interrupted by teachers and the many resources of the school were not categorized as play resources, as they could be used for teacher-led activities.

The plan was for topics of learning to be determined by children and operationalized by teachers. Children in neither country commented on this point. Children in Scotland seemed to have accepted that a primary school, where five year olds in their country can be found, had the primary aim to teach the specific elements they mentioned. On the contrary, children in Greece commented on (a) play and child initiated activities and (b) their safety. Children in Greece discussed only the elements of a kindergarten they wanted to be changed in the plan to agree with the way it functioned in their country. Therefore, children in Scotland emphasized that learning academic stuff is appropriate for children of their age whereas children in Greece had accepted that a safe and play based school was appropriate for them. Children in Scotland prioritized children right to education (article 28.1) and in particular, the education of children in relation to the development of mental and physical abilities / capabilities (article 29(a)) and partly with children preparation for a responsible life in a free society (article 29(d)). Children in Greece emphasized article 31 on their right to play, when discussing the physical environment of a school for young children.

The Social Environment Of A School

Scotland

Valley School

Children had a wider definition of rules than the one I had in mind when writing the plan. I aimed to start a conversation about classroom rules but they talked about them as well as school rules and regulations.

ES: You know, in this school the children want to decide the rules together with their teachers. How do you feel about that?

Good.

ES: Good? Did you decide the classroom rules with your teacher?

Em ... no.

ES: No, but would you have liked that?

Yeah.

Yeah.

ES: What rules would you tell her to have or change?

Em ... Maybe we could, if you are still hungry, we could, we could tell the dinner, lunch people that we need more lunch.

ES: Ok. So, you are allowed just one plate, one tray and not a second one. No second helpings.

Em ... yes.

ES: What about other rules? Rules about behavior and things like that.

No hitting and pushing.

Or punching.

ES: No punching? Ok.

Em ... they could learn some more things and learn to have schoolbags and marbles.

ES: And ... what did you say?

Bring schoolbag with stuff like water bottles and snacks.

ES: Water bottles. So, you want water bottles in school, different bags. Alright. Different bags when you say not those, not the school ones. You don't like the school bags.

Well, we do like our schoolbags but we just, I just want to get a new one so that we can see if some things fit in it. And the children can get some more play time like star time and come to play and see if they are allowed to go the beach.

ES: Alright. More time to play and visits to the beach.

And allowed to swim if they have a swimming suit.

ES: What if they have a swimming suit, but they don't know how to swim?

They could learn how to swim or another friend of them can help them.

These children liked the idea of deciding their rules with their teachers, which is a matter affecting them, as article 12 foresees. They also suggested topics of discussion about rules and regulations in their school and of decisions with their teachers. Uniformity imposed by school policy (one type of school bag and one portion of food only), whether it was due to Valley School policy or primary education policy in Scotland, seemed to bother these children. They wanted more play time in Valley School and more contact with the world outside their school but in the company of their peers, such as visits to the seaside. However, children were not allowed or did not know of a way of raising these issues with adults in their school. They connected their right of being seriously consulted to (a) their safety (article 19), as they wanted rules to protect children from other children harming them physically and to (b) play (article 31).

This group was also asked their views about children co-deciding with their teachers about any issue other than rules. As they did not reply, I brought the question to a more realistic framework rather than using the plan to facilitate the discussion. By doing so, children talked and said they wanted to change their daily schedule. They were not clear about on what activities time would be spent in their new schedule, except perhaps writing. They also wanted different reading books, new reading material from sources other than school books as well as more input in mathematics. They were very interested in language and mathematics but also in real-life texts rather than only those written by adults for children. All the above mean that children wanted to co-decide with teachers on issues related to their academic learning and their safety.

Fire safety was another matter of interest to them and they wanted to know more about it. These children mentioned fire protection just like children in the authoritarian school group from the same school so perhaps this was an issue in Valley School at the time.

ES: Would you like children to decide something with teachers?

No.

ES: No? You want them to decide for you?

I'd like to decide with teachers.

ES: What would you like to decide with your teachers? About what?

About time?

About time. What do you mean? What you are going to do?

Yeah.

ES: Alright. Ok. So, change the routine.

Yeah.

And maybe they [the children in the plan] could learn to fight. But not fight each other. Fight dragons if there is one in the school.

And [learn to fight] in case there is a fire.

ES: Ok. How about what Bret said? Would you like to decide something with your teacher?

Well, yeah.

What?

The same as Bret.

ES: Alright. So, the daily routine. What would you change in the daily routine then? What would you tell your teacher to change?

I might change our reading books and do a little bit more writing.

ES: Ok. So, more writing? Ok.

Maybe we could we could, we could get real life stories and see if we can read them.

ES: Real life stories and see if you can read them? Ok. Christine? Would like to decide something with your teacher?

Yeah.

ES: What would you like to talk to her about?

Emm...Maths.

ES: Maths. What would you tell your teacher about Maths?

We maybe can do a bigger worksheet.

Children raised the issues they wanted to be consulted about in their own schools. Article 12 was related to children's right to education (articles 28.1 - 29(a)) in terms of content (*e.g.* different books) and quantity (*e.g.* more mathematics and writing). Children appreciated having an education but they could not inform teachers about their needs or tastes so that their teaching could suit them better. The importance of implementing article 5 of the Convention became obvious.

Greece

Children from all three schools of the sample did not elaborate on the issue of rules being decided both by children and teachers but thought it was a good idea. Children in Elm School were in favor of rules being co-decided between teachers and children but their views about it varied between the groups of Oak School and Pine Schools. As for deciding about other school matters with their teachers, children in all three groups were in favor of it.

Elm School

This group wanted their teachers to consult them whether it was about rule setting or any other matter in school.

ES: So is it better to discuss everything all together?

Yes.

Yes.

ES: And the classroom rules to discuss together?

Yes.

ES: So you think it is a good idea for the teacher and the children to decide together about rules?

Yes.

Children did not seem to have much to say but the steadiness in their answers could be said to indicate a liking of the idea behind article 12 of the Convention.

ES: Well, I want to ask you, is this the plan for the best school ever or not?

Did the children decide?

ES: Yes, the children decided with their teacher.

The best school ever!

ES: So, is it better for the children and their teacher to decide together?

(It's) better because when the teachers decide (on their own), children say no and we do not know what to do.

At the end of the session, I asked:

ES: So, you said that you want little children to decide together with their teachers about everything.

Yes, if we decide together about everything, everything will be resolved and they (children) will not be naughty.

ES: Can you tell me what you would like to decide with your teacher?

I cannot.

I do not know what.

Me neither.

Me neither.

ES: *Then why do you say that you want children to decide together with their teacher?*

(Because) I want to.

ES: *You want to decide. About what?*

I need to think about it.

I think that children and teachers should think together. Children know some things and teachers know some others. And when they discuss them, they will find solutions together. This way all problems will be solved and children will not be naughty.

ES: *Yes.*

Once together with Mrs. Anne we decided that we will do a play.

ES: *Oh, and did you like that? Deciding with her about what you are going to do, just like the plan said?*

Yes.

Their further discussion indicated that they wanted to be consulted by their teachers even though they did not know on what topics decisions had to be made or even though they did not have a topic of interest in mind. It sounds a lot more like they wanted to be included and their views considered when decisions are to be made affecting them. Children's views show that, apart from the significance of article 12, the implementation of children's right to appropriate direction and guidance in the exercise of their right to be consulted (article 5) was necessary.

Oak School

As for co-deciding about rules with their teachers, some children within the same group said yes and some no, but all of them could not or would not explain their answers or discussed the topic further. Only a child in Oak School justified her answer by explaining that the teacher runs the school so she decides the rules in her classroom. This was so powerful that made the other child retract her statement that she likes the idea of children co-deciding the rules with their teachers.

ES: In this school children will decide the rules with their teachers. How do you feel about it?

I do not like it.

I like it.

ES: Why do you say that (do not like it)?

Because the teacher runs the school.

ES: Why would you want to decide on rules with your teacher?

I was only joking.

Rule setting was either the teacher's duty or a topic for children to be consulted, so article 12 was important but not to all of them. For some children, perhaps the feature of low individualism of the national culture in Greece, which means that children depend on adults without much encouragement for independence, influenced their views. This makes the implementation of article 5 on children's right to guidance in exercising their rights more urgent, so that children can enjoy their right to participation in decision-making (article 12).

However, when asked more generally about children co-deciding about any issue with their teachers, their answers indicated the significance of article 12 to these children more strongly. This group stated that they would like children to decide with their teachers but they could not justify their response. They agreed with the idea of deciding about establishing new schools, about outings and punishments with their teachers but they could not discuss it further.

ES: Do you like the idea of children deciding with the teacher?

Yes.

ES: If you were allowed to decide something with your teacher, what would that be?

The yes.

ES: *What does the yes mean?*

I would say yes to their making kindergartens.

ES: *Would you have liked to decide with your teacher if you were to go on excursions or what to do with children that do not behave well?*

Yes.

This inability or reluctance to discuss decision-making further may be an indicator of the need for better provision for the implementation of article 5. Children liked and agreed with the idea of co-deciding (article 12) but they did not have anything further to add, indicating the possibility that their evolving capacities needed direction and guidance on their teacher's part (article 5).

Pine School

Children in this school held views similar to those held by children from Oak School. In Pine School, however, views about how to decide the rules were split according to gender. Boys said they wanted to decide with their teacher whereas for girls setting the rules was part of the teacher's work. They did not add anything further.

ES: *Would you like to decide about the rules with the teacher?*

No.

Yes.

ES: *You would not? Who should decide? The teacher on her own?*

She nods yes.

You boys? What did you say? You with the teacher?

Yes.

However, the significance that article 12 had for all children in the group became evident when asked directly about deciding with their teachers about matters in general.

ES: So tell me, would you have liked what the children said? To decide about things with their teacher?

Yes.

ES: If you could decide with your teacher what would you decide about?

We decide about games.

ES: How about some things about the school, like the rules, should you decide them with your teacher?

Yes.

Children were not very talkative. They liked the idea of deciding with their teachers in general. Their answers indicate that rules at school was perhaps something some of these children believed had to be set by adults on their own.

Comparison Of Children's Views On The Social Environment

Children in Valley School in Scotland and in Elm School in Greece agreed on children setting the rules together with their teachers. Children's views from Oak School and Pine School in Greece were split between rules being set only by the teacher and rules being set by the teacher with the children. The low score on individualism according to Hofstede (2021b) may explain why some children did not consider participation in rule setting as a matter for them to co-decide.

All children in both countries wanted children to decide about matters other than rule setting with their teachers. This means that they appreciated article 12 but only children from Scotland had topics for decision-making to suggest to their teachers. The significance of article 5 about children's right to guidance by teachers to exercise their rights was raised.

NOTES

[1] The teacher will ask the children what they want to do and learn and that is what they will do.

CHAPTER 7

The Perfect School for Wilson

Abstract: In the second focus group session of this research, each group of children read the beginning of a book called *Whiffy Wilson, the wolf who wouldn't go to school*. In this chapter, children's perceptions of the perfect school for Wilson are presented. Children in both countries suggested a school where play time would be allowed a lot more than in their schools. Sugar-based foods were more popular in Scotland than in Greece, which disagrees with children's right to healthy nutrition (article 24). Children in all groups from Scotland discussed learning in terms of the education they were being offered, and they wanted help for Wilson or no lessons at all nor a teacher for him. On the contrary, most of the groups in Greece did not talk about learning in school. Friendships were important to children in Greece only, even though all children in both countries discussed classroom rules that would enable positive relations with other children.

Keywords: Indulgence, Individualism, Power distance, Right to education, Right to participation, Right to play, Right to safety.

INTRODUCTION

In this section, the data from the second focus group sessions with children are analyzed. In our second session, the children were read the following part of the book called *Whiffy Wilson, the wolf who wouldn't go to school* (Hart, 2014).

There was a wolf called Wilson who couldn't count to ten. He wouldn't learn to write his name. He never used a pen. He didn't know his A B Cs. He couldn't paint or cook. He wouldn't learn his two-plus-twos. He never read a book.

'Time for school!' his father cried, 'you pesky little pup!'.

'But school is BORING!' Wilson whined, and he turned the telly up.

One morning, Wilson went next door to ask his friend to play. But Dotty smiled, 'I can't because I'm off to school today.'

Evanthia Synodi
All rights reserved-© 2023 Bentham Science Publishers

'Well, I'm not going', Wilson grumped. 'Who wants to read and write? I'd rather play and watch TV and stay up late at night.'

'Oh, you're so silly', Dotty smiled. 'Come to school with me! There's nothing to be scared of - school's lots of fun, you'll see!'

'WHO SAYS I'M SCARED?' growled Wilson. 'A wolf is brave and strong. It's just ... the teacher might be cross if I get the answers wrong.'

Children were then asked to suggest what school would make Wilson want to attend it. The data about a school for Wilson are presented first for each country in terms of physical and social environment and then the data from Scotland and Greece are compared.

Scotland

In Scotland, there were two groups from Valley School who discussed the story of Wilson. For their second focus group session, it was not possible to group children from Valley School with the criterion of having discussed the same plan in their first session. A girl in group MX1 was not present in the first session as well as a boy in MX2. Both groups were comprised of five children. In Hill School, on the other hand, the groups remained the same as in their first session.

Valley School MX1

Children from Valley School who participated in this session had suggestions only for the social environment of the perfect school for Wilson. Resources, time and space for play were not mentioned at all in their descriptions.

Social Environment

This group emphasized other children's behavior, *i.e.* Wilson's classmates' behavior, as a motive for him to go to school. They said that other children should be '*nice*' to him and play and share stuff with Wilson. They discussed the teacher's behavior, too. The teacher should be nice to him, like his classmates should, and encourage them to be nice to Wilson. She (the teacher) should give him his school equipment and teach him both the basics and not to neglect his diet.

ES: What sort of school, do you think, can make Wilson to want to go to school?

If people were nice to one another and share with them.

ES: Okay. What else?

Maybe if they could give him a school bag and a water bottle and a pencil case and things that you need for school.

ES: Okay. So, a school where they give you all the stuff you need for learning like school bags and things and where people are nice. Anything else?

Maybe we could make him feel to go to school.

ES: How?

To play nicely.

ES: Play nicely! Nelly, any ideas?

Maybe a wolf school?

ES: A wolf school! And what would the wolf school be like?

Nobody answers.

ES: Would it be wrong if he went to school with Dotty?

Again nobody answers.

ES: you think he would be more comfortable with other wolves?

Yeah [he would be].

ES: You think he would be more comfortable with other wolves?

She nods yes.

They may even talk better when he is at school. The teacher might say "Everybody, be really nice to the wolf!"

ES: So a nice teacher as well! Any other ideas?

No.

ES: No ideas about what school? Okay. What would the school look like then?

It might look like a place that teachers are nice to some (of the) people who haven't been to school and they are learning about ABCs and 1, 2, 3s and trying to eat their food all up.

These children did not refer to play resources but referred to a rule about how to play, which was to play 'nicely'. They did not give details of what nicely means. However, this view can be related to article 31 (children's right to play) and article 29(b) on the children's right to an education on human rights and partially with article 29(d) on education that teaches them understanding, peace, tolerance, equality of sexes and friendships with other people. The significance of their right to education (articles 28.1 and 29(a)) was also indicated in their wanting children and Wilson to learn the 3R's in school.

Being *nice* to others and sharing stuff with them are behaviors that can facilitate children's right to association (article 15). They are also in accordance with the Preamble of the Convention which refers to children's right to having their dignity respected. If one considers their opposites *i.e.* being horrible to others and not sharing, it is evident that their views were also in agreement with children's right to protection from physical and mental harm (article 19). The adjective nice, that was used four times, and the adverb nicely, that was used once, were terms all the children used in this session. It appears to describe co-existing without disruptions and having and keeping a common and homogeneous perspective on how to be teachers and peers / classmates. Having seen their classroom rules written and exhibited on one of the classroom walls, I can confirm that they also included the term nice.

The children did not mention anything specific regarding resources, time and space for play for the perfect school for Wilson. However, they mentioned that Wilson and his classmates should have the opportunity to play together. The only reference made about the physical environment of the perfect school for Wilson had to do with Wilson being a pupil. Children believed that a school which will make Wilson want to attend it should provide him with a pupil's equipment, such as a water bottle, a pencil case, and a school bag. This in relation to children and Wilson learning the 3R's indicates that children right to an education (articles 28 and 29) is a major consideration for these children when describing the perfect school for Wilson.

Valley School MX2

These children focused mainly on satisfying Wilson's habits as described in the excerpt of the book I read to them. They had suggestions both for the physical and the social environment of the best school for Wilson.

Physical Environment

This group wanted a television in school, no academic work (in the form of doing writing or story work), lots of toys for Wilson to play with and a servant to do things for him. They also added Wilson eating unhealthy food, such as sweets and crisps.

ES: So, what sort of school would make Wilson to want to go to school?

A school where they're playing or only watch TV.

And he could eat sweets and crisps all day.

ES: Eat sweet things and crisps. Anything else? What kind of school would make him want to go?

Where he could play?

But Christine said that.

ES: Yes, Christine said that. Anything else?

No.

A school with lots of toys in it?

ES: Lots of toys in it.

No writing.

ES: No writing, you say. What would the school look like?

It would look like it's made of bricks.

ES: Made of bricks? Okay. How about the yard?

Grass.

With toys in the yard.

ES: What kind of toys in the yard?

Toys, just random toys.

Flowers in the yard.

For the perfect school for Wilson, these children believed that children's right to play and leisure (article 31) must be respected and fulfilled to the detriment of Wilson's right to education (articles 28-29), as they wanted him to play all day. Therefore, this group commented on the time and resources of play, which should be a lot, but not on the required space for it. As they mentioned the need for flora in the schoolyard, contact with nature was important to them so much as to include it in the best school for Wilson. This forms a strong basis for education for respect for the natural environment (article 29(e)). Unhealthy food was also desirable in a school for Wilson and against article 24 of the Convention, which foresees children's right to health in terms of nutrition.

Social Environment

Children did not mention the role of the teacher and they could not discuss the classroom rules for the perfect school for Wilson. The only rule mentioned was about Wilson's movement. A boy suggested that Wilson be allowed to run or walk everywhere and a girl suggested walking as a condition of safety.

ES: And what about his teacher or the classroom rules? What kind of rules would he like to have in the school?

Tim[1]: Run in the school.

ES: Okay. When you say running in school, what do you mean?

Like he could run everywhere.

ES: Alright. So, why do you think he would like that?

Well, I'm not sure.

ES: *Why did you say it?*

Nobody comments.

ES: *I would like to talk a little bit more about running in school. You, Tim, said he would like that. Do the rest of you agree?*

No.

Yeah.

ES: *Okay. Why not? Why not, Elisa?*

He might fall over or he might bump into something.

ES: *Okay. So, what you are saying is that the safe thing would be to walk ...*

Yeah.

ES: *Rather than run in the school.*

Yeah, because if you are running and someone is slower than you, you may bump into them.

Nobody comments. Tim does not defend his position.

Tim probably thought of wolves in the wild where they run, which Wilson would not be able to do in school, as Elisa explained. Tim's idea had to do with respecting one's nature, which is in accordance with article 29(a) about children's rights to education that develops their physical abilities but respects differences, which is in accordance with article 2 and children's right not to be discriminated. However, Elisa, too, considered differences in physical abilities between human pupils and animal pupils (article 29(a)), such as speed, and suggested a rule about everyone's safety, respecting article 19.

I asked a probing question to check for more ideas since the children could not further discuss pupils' speed of movement in school.

ES: Okay. Have you got any other ideas about the school he would like?

I think he would like somebody to do everything for him, like hang his bag, hang his coat up.

I would like that.

ES: Anything else?

I think a servant.

A servant! Yes. That's right.

Children views took into consideration Wilson's wish not to go to a school where he would have to do work. However, hanging coats and bags was not something Wilson complained about in the story. They did not show any concern about Wilson's right to education (articles 28-29) and they even suggested he had a servant at school. The thought of the servant for Wilson and children liking the idea of a servant for themselves could be explained in two ways. It could be due to the high score of indulgence in the UK society as defined by Hofstede (2019b), which means that children wanted gratification of their drive to have fun but not the responsibilities that come with it. It could also be because the environment, the structure and the operation of their primary school were not appropriate for them. Perhaps the transition from nursery school to Primary 1 was not smooth and the differences between the two institutions were too great for them to handle.

Hill School AU

When asked what school would make Wilson attend it, children in Hill School talked about (a) all sorts of resources related to play, (b) food, (c) learning and (d) teachers' behavior. Their suggestions seemed to be a combination of the education they received, whether acceptable to them or not, and the character of Wilson, as described in the excerpt. In accordance with the book, for example, they suggested having a television in school to cater to Wilson's idiosyncrasies but they also added chocolates and sweets. However, the book excerpt read to them did not mention anything about Wilson's eating habits, whereas these children were not allowed sugary products in their school.

Physical Environment

Toys, televisions, flower gardens, water slides, computer games, slides, pets, books, chocolates, cakes, strawberries and a school close to his house were characteristics of a school that Wilson would like to attend.

ES: *What do you think this school should be like so that Wilson will want to go?*

Umm, lots of toys?

Yeah.

Yes.

A TV?

ES: *Toys, a TV, yes. What else?*

A flower garden.

Oh yes, with the flowers.

A water flower slide?

ES: *Why do you think he would want them?*

Because they would be fun to smell.

ES: *Mmm, so, you think Wilson would want something fun to smell. What else do you think Wilson would want?*

A computer.

ES: *Why do you think he would want a computer?*

So he can play a game.

ES: *Play games, okay.*

Have a slide that you go down.

ES: *Slides.*

Just a little one.

Umm, a big cat in school?

ES: A big cat?

A pet.

ES: A pet cat. Okay.

Books.

A water fountain.

Or a chocolate fountain!

Strawberries.

And a strawberry and a chocolate cake.

To this group, children's right to play (article 31) was important. Children made references only to resources relevant to play but not to the time and space allocated to play while at school. An educational environment with fauna and flora was also of interest to them, which in its turn can enable the implementation of article 29(e). Food was necessary, too, but apart from strawberries, their suggestions were against article 24 and children right to healthy food.

Social Environment

One girl[2] did not want any teacher at the school for Wilson; she wanted him to be allowed to do whatever he wants, as adults do, in her opinion. Another girl wanted a teacher who would not make rules for the children on her own. When I asked them to further describe the perfect school, they described a school where Wilson would learn to write his own name and read books, sing and rest.

ES What kind of teacher do you think he would want?

No teacher.

He would like a nice teacher who doesn't make rules on her own.

ES: What else would make Wilson want to go to school?

He could learn to write his own name and read books.

I think he wishes that he is a grown-up, so that he can do whatever he likes.

ES: He wants to be a grown-up, so, he wants to do whatever he likes?

Or he could sing songs and listen to songs and go to sleep.

ES: Is that what grown-ups do or is that the kind of school he wants?

The kind of school he wants.

Sing songs and go to bed.

ES: Oh, a bed.

Children's right to education (articles 28 and 29) and children's right to be consulted when rules are set for them (article 12) were important aspects of a school for Wilson as well as article 31 on the children's right to rest. However, one of the girls was not satisfied with that. She thought that, since Wilson does whatever he wants at home, a primary school with teachers and work is not an environment he would like. This could be so, because she sympathized with Wilson and respected his idiosyncrasies. However, it could be that she felt that primary teachers with their assignments were not what she herself needed. Perhaps primary school work was too much for her and she did not want Wilson to go through that. Such a perception can also be related to the high score of indulgence characterizing the UK culture.

Hill School DP

Children in this group commented mainly on resources and time for play (*e.g.* waterpark and disco time) for the best school for Wilson. Eating sweets and other sugar based snacks was also considered important for Wilson, even though the excerpt read to them did not mention anything about food. However, such food was prohibited at their school. A more flexible, relaxed atmosphere was also essential for a school for Wilson.

The Physical Environment

For the perfect school for Wilson, play resources and sugar-based food were the children priorities, emphasizing article 31 and devaluing article 24 of the Convention.

ES: So, I was wondering, do you have any idea about what kind of school would make Wilson want to go to school?

Waterpark.

ES: A school with a waterpark.

Fire slides.

ES: With a fire slide. Okay.

All of it to be play time.

ES: Play time? All of it to be play time? Is that what you said?

They could still learn ... they can still learn outside so they could still ... at the same time do playtime and learning.

ES: Learning outside while playing. Yes?

Yeah.

Well, they could do Maths outside and play out at the same time.

That's the same thing I said.

ES: Yes. Anne agrees with you.

What about lots of star[3] time like two star times a day?

ES: Two golden times a day! Okay.

And they lasted for two hours.

ES: Two hours each. Okay. Anything else?

And they had big sales every single day.

ES: Selling what?

Cakes.

Chocolate things.

Biscuits.

Cakes and ice lollies for the bake sales.

ES: Okay. Bake sales then. Anything else?

No.

A little later, they added further play resources and time for play as well as repeated wanting unhealthy food in school.

I think every day the choice should be if you would like to play outside all day or stay inside and have a disco.

I think the choice should be to be able to have …

A chocolate.

Or a chocolate lollipop in his class.

ES: Alright.

Or a mint - choc ice cream in class.

Or a fat ice cream.

I've had it before. It's delicious!

I think they should have it only on Halloween. They should have parties and every single day I think they should have a birthday party for each person.

ES: Anne, you're only like 25 people in the class. So, that's 25 birthdays.

Yeah.

ES: You mean those 25? Okay.

And water fights!

And water fights!

Water fights with water guns.

And water pistols.

There should be eight Halloweens, everyone should be dancing away.

ES: Anything else?

I think there should be, in a school, a giant room that had lots and lots of toys in it.

ES: A room with toys.

I think each desk should have a special big robot rubber that's in the middle, coming out of a hole and you just need to press a button put in front of you and the robot rubber comes and rubs out anything you've done wrong so you wouldn't need to be scrub, scrub, scrub with the rubber and then it's gone!

ES: So, you want a robot to clean after you?

Uh huh.

Article 31 on children's right to play was the most important right to be respected by the best school for Wilson. Children had a different perception of education, which included learning while playing or no learning similar to the one they were experiencing. Article 28 was appreciated and a discrepancy between the children's own school experiences and aspects of a child friendly education according to article 29 was expressed.

Children also mentioned unhealthy food as necessary, even though it is against their right to healthy nutrition (article 24). Furthermore, children wanted a robot for Wilson and themselves to do things for them. Children cleaning after themselves was not popular, in a way similar to what the children from Valley School MX2 said. Children either felt primary school was not as child friendly and child centered as they needed it to be or, as a child new to school, Wilson would enjoy to school would enjoy. It could also be due to the high score of indulgence, which characterizes the UK culture.

Social Environment

For Wilson, children wanted a teacher who would do silly things themselves and allow children to do so as well; a teacher who would not make him 'work' and who would let him play and dance. The distinction between work / teacher organized activities and play / child initiated activities was clear in these children's views lending support to research findings by Wood (2010) and Howard (2010).

ES: What kind of teacher do you think he would like?

A teacher that's so crazy that he would let us do silly things.

A teacher ... that smack their heads on the table!

Ha, ha ...

ES: Oh sorry I didn't understand what you mean.

Like, I mean, like a really silly teacher, not like Mrs Smith[4]. Crazy and smack the table.

ES: The teacher would smack the table?

They do this, bam, bam, bam!

ES: Teachers do that, smacking their heads.

Yeah, and letting everyone blow raspberries.

ES: What does this mean?

That means like that ... (child making blowing sound with mouth).

ES: Okay. Alright. So, that's why you said not like Mrs Smith because she is more serious.

She is still a nice teacher, but she gets us to do work.

ES: And that teacher [of the perfect school] doesn't. Oh, so you think that Wilson would prefer a teacher that doesn't make him work.

Yeah.

Yeah.

Yeah.

Yeah, he could just play around all day.

He could have a disco three times a day for like nine hours.

A disco three times a day, to last for every single year.

These children believed that they worked too hard and that they should not, therefore, they did not want the same for Wilson. They believed they did not play enough in school and they did not want that for Wilson. They believed the repertoire of acceptable behaviors for pupils was limited and they were not allowed to be as playful as they needed or wanted to at school. For this reason, they did not want Wilson to experience the same and suggested a teacher more lax than the teachers in their school. This was confirmed by the rules and behaviors they suggested for Wilson's school, such as not tidying up and his being allowed to do what he wants, as well as by the physical environment of the school with pictures of toilets on the walls, in and out of school.

ES: Okay. What kind of rules do you think he would like to have in the school?

No walking around.

No walking around.

No walking around.

No walking allowed.

ES: No walking allowed. I think you are joking, Jack. If he is not allowed to walk then he would have to sit all day!

No.

He could skip and hop.

He could ride a giant bicycle to the roof.

And go up the stairs with a bicycle and come back down.

ES: So, rules would be: no walking.

Yes, no walking.

ES: Okay. Anything else?

No, no, no, no, there should be no coming in from outside.

ES: Okay. So, they should be outside all day.

Yeah.

Yeah.

Oh, no.

The teacher forgets to tell the class to tidy up for star time.

Yeah.

Yeah.

We could have pictures of toilets on the walls.

Or, like, (pictures of toilets) up in the playground.

And you could do whatever you want.

Children's description of the ideal teacher for Wilson, of the classroom rules and of the features of the school environment showed that they thought Wilson needed more time for play and in particular physical play with more use of his body (*e.g.* disco time, riding a bicycle, water fights and skipping and hopping) allowed in school than they were offered. A strict teacher, lack of resources, both in terms of toys and play facilities, and lack of time for play were not appreciated. A distance between teacher and children, which does not allow playfulness to grow in school, was not welcome.

Initially children mentioned learning through playing outside as well as lots of time to play. As the discussion progressed, they changed and added a teacher who does not make Wilson work hard and then a teacher who lets Wilson play and have fun only. Their recommendations for people blowing raspberries, teachers' smacking their own heads, pictures of toilets indoors and outdoors show that these children may have needed a less strict environment in school. In combination, these two desirable features of a school for Wilson perhaps show a discrepancy between these children life at home and the expectations of a school from them or between childhood as experienced in and out of school.

Children did not want Wilson to work at all or to work hard at school or to be in a class where children are responsible for themselves and tidy up. This may indicate that their education was not as child-centered and child friendly as it should have been in order to cater for them in accordance with article 29 of the Convention and GC 7 2005. However, it could be a sign of the high score of indulgence as defined by Hofstede (2019b) in the UK. It is also in accordance with the societal tendency for easy money and for little work with little difficulty.

Comparison of Data within Scotland

In this section of the chapter, the findings from Scotland about the perfect school for Wilson are analyzed. Four groups of children from Scotland participated in focus group sessions discussing the excerpt from the book *Whiffy Wilson the wolf who wouldn't go to school*.

Children from the Valley MX1 group did not refer to the physical environment of the school at all. All the remaining groups suggested sweets and play resources for the perfect school for Wilson. Valley MX2 and Hill DP also required more time for play on top of more resources for it. Two groups (Valley MX2 and Hill AU) would add flowers to the plan for a school for him. Views on learning and working in school were split as two groups would omit learning and work (Valley MX2 and Hill DP) in the perfect school for Wilson whereas Valley MX1 and Hill AU wanted Wilson to learn subjects like the 3R's at school.

When it comes to the social environment of the perfect school for Wilson, children from Hill AU did not wish the school for Wilson to have a teacher but if it did, they preferred the teacher not to make the classroom rules on her own. Children from Hill DP described a mockery of teacher, a person that has no reason or responsibility. Children from Hill DP extended the word crazy from the teacher to the rules of the classroom.

As for the rules of acceptable behavior, children from Valley MX1 described general behaviors employing the terms used at their school. The word nice and nicely accompanied children's and Wilson's playing, sharing and being with others.

Children's views from Scotland indicate a pattern in their perception of the perfect school for Wilson. Three out of the four groups adopted a similar rationale when imagining the perfect school for Wilson, which is based on what the children considered overwhelming or undesirable in Primary 1 classes, that is, the multitude of tasks for children to do, decided and assigned to them by adults without any consideration for children feelings or views or even needs, such as play.

Children from Valley School MX2 and from Hill School DP respectively wanted a servant and a robot to do things for Wilson and for themselves at school. To them, children are expected to do a lot at school, which is too tiring. In relation to that, some children from Hill School AU expressed the opinion that a school without teachers would be best for Wilson, so that he could do whatever he wished. Their fellow pupils in Hill School DP wanted a teacher who would behave like children do, when they are oppressed. It is not academic learning and skill that seemed to bother children in school because they suggested the 3R's and singing as aspects of the perfect school for Wilson. However, they must have been overwhelmed by the expectations for a primary school pupil, as they wanted somebody else to do part of their work or even to be allowed to do whatever they want, no matter how silly.

This explanation is reinforced by their suggestions for play equipment and time for play for the perfect school for Wilson. Opportunities for play for Wilson are on par with a more relaxed school atmosphere, which satisfies the reason for funny teachers and rude or ridiculous pictures on the wall *etc.* It is also in accordance with their suggestion of Wilson be allowed to eat unhealthy food in school. There may be many explanations for the fact that unhealthy food was essential. However, the disparity between home and school diet was very strong for these children. In any case, children were not consulted but obligated to eat healthy food at school in accordance with article 24 of the Convention but apparently not with the child-centered methodology of GC 7 2005 or article 12 of the Convention.

All groups, but MX1, indicate that the indulgence and power distance scores of the UK do not correspond to children perceptions. It seems that the power distance, that is, the unequal to other people in the UK position of these children did not allow them the degree of indulgence they wished for.

Only one group, Valley School MX1, gave answers about the perfect school for Wilson, which do not indicate any connection with disagreement or dissatisfaction with the provision and the practices they experienced at school. They did not discuss the physical environment of the school but they mentioned pupil's equipment (*e.g.* school bags). They were also in favor of Wilson learning reading and writing. These children's suggestions had to do with behavior among the participants in education when children and Wilson are taught. Valley School MX1 was the only group of children who did not indicate that they felt that power distance in the UK decreased their degree of indulgence.

Greece

Elm School AU

When discussing the physical environment of the perfect school for Wilson, these children prioritized article 31 on children's right to play.

The Physical Environment

The first remarks about a perfect school for Wilson that children made were about play resources, such as trains, legos, hoops, slides, cars, and dolls. They would also include small animals, such as puppies, and trees in the schoolyard of this perfect school for him.

ES: What do you think he would like in a school?

Toys.

We should have (toy) trains.

Legos.

Hoops.

(Toy) kitchen.

Yes, he may want to be a chef.

ES: Anything else?

Slides.

Little toy cars.

A yard with animals.

ES: What animals should this kindergarten have?

Small ones. In an area surrounded by a fence so that we can see them.

It should have a trampoline.

Puppies.

Plush or real?

Real.

ES: Will you take care of the puppy so that it can live at school?

Yes, I would put it to bed, give it a pacifier and put pants on it.

ES: What else should it have?

Beach umbrellas.

A board.

It should have boxes of dolls.

And playmobils.

A library, too.

Trees for the children to climb.

Playhouses with doors and steps out to the yard.

These answers indicate the importance of play for a school for Wilson and young children and thus of their right to play (article 31). This group did not mention anything about time and space for play. They also included flora and fauna, which means that children's right to education cultivating respect for the natural environment (article 29(e)) was likely to be facilitated.

The Social Environment

Children made comments on the ideal teacher for Wilson. On top of not telling children off, they wanted a teacher who would make children happy by bringing them new resources (*e.g.* trampolines, dresses) to play with, which were missing in their own kindergarten. They were the only children out of all the children in both countries who connected children happiness in school to their teachers in their discussions of a perfect school for Wilson.

ES: And what about the teacher?

A very good one.

ES: What does a very good teacher mean?

Not to tell off the children that beat others, we can simply talk about it.

ES: What else should the teacher do so that it is nice when at school?

She should make children happy.

ES: How can she make children happy?

She can bring a trampoline at school.

And dresses for the girls (for dress up).

A good teacher for Wilson is somebody who does not scold children even when they are mean to other children and somebody who finds ways to make children happy at school. Telling children off is not the right way for a teacher to handle misbehavior; talking about mistakes is, according to this group.

When I asked the children about rules, they talked about rules that protect Wilson from physical abuse from others and rules about keeping the classroom clean and neat.

ES: What rules should it (the school) have to make Wilson want to go to school?

To tidy up.

To sweep.

Not to beat others, not to pinch them.

Not to kick them, not to slap them.

Not to fight.

Children wanted Wilson to learn how to be responsible and self-reliant, which is in accordance with children's right to an education that prepares children for a responsible life (article 29(d)) as well as with their right to be protected from harm (article 19).

Elm School RB

The girls in this group were in favor of Wilson going to school with the children. They could accept the idea that a wolf can go to a kindergarten, even though neither I nor the book made such a distinction between children and wolves when reading them the story or posing questions. However, they were divided in their views about the perfect school for Wilson both in terms of school layout and of resources.

Physical Environment

In terms of layout, two of the girls wanted one building with classrooms for different species of animals / pupils, whereas the other two wanted a different building for each species (humans and wolves) but with a common schoolyard for both schools.

ES: What school do you think would make Wilson want to go?

A kindergarten.

ES: Which would look like what?

Like a school with wolves.

ES: Only with wolves?

Page: And little children.

ES: Would it have anything else?

A day nursery.

A playground.

ES: A playground and a day nursery for the younger puppies and the younger children. Would it have a teacher?

It would have to because otherwise what would happen to so many children, doggies, kittens, puppies?

ES: What would the teacher be?

A dog teacher, a lady teacher, a wolf teacher!

ES: So, this school will have three different classrooms?

Yes.

ES: And in one [classroom] only the little wolves would go, and in other only the little children?

So that they do not fight.

Then the other two girls start talking about something else.

But again they are together (children and animals) and they may fight. We can put them a little further away.

ES: What do you mean to put them a little further away?

We will detach one school from the other.

ES: So, in which would Wilson want to go?

In kindergarten.

ES: With other little wolves or with other little children?

With little wolves.

I think we should have one school on this side and another one on the other.

I was going to say the same thing.

And they can meet at breaks (with Dotty) and give the little girl (Dotty) the right answers (to her teachers' questions).

So then I asked the other two girls what they thought and they replied:

ES: What do you think, do you like this idea?

I do not like it.

ES: Why not?

I like Page's idea.

ES: So what would this school (you prefer) be like?

One school with one classroom just for the wolves.

ES: And what else would it [the perfect kindergarten] have?

Little wolves would like to eat sweets and the teacher should let them.

ES: Whereas little children?

Little children would like toys, playhouses, toy animals ...

ES: So, little wolves would not want playhouses and toys. So, let me get this straight. You want a school just for wolves where Wilson can attend. And would it have toys inside?

Yes.

Sweets.

It [the school] will have sweets in it.

Yes, little animals are one (thing), little children are another[5].

ES: And what sort of yard should they have?

They will have a yard with drawings.

The yard on the little wolves' side should have toys, and playhouses with doors and they will be there and play and have fun. And to have a trampoline.

ES: What else would you like it to have?

To have his mum and dad painted.

ES: To have somebody paint his mum and dad?

Yes.

ES: On the wall?

Yes.

Slides.

ES: The yard to have slides?

And potato crisps.

A playground was important for both plans suggested for a school for Wilson. Wolves would need sweets, meat and their yard to have trampolines and paintings on the walls outside, slides and according to half of the children, playhouses and other toys. Children attending this school, on the other hand, would need toy animals. Children suggestions indicate that their right to play (article 31) was important to them, even though they did not mention anything about time and space for play. Unhealthy foods, such as sweets and crisps, were included but they are not on a par with article 24.

In a way, both school layouts children suggested for Wilson seemed to be based on their understanding of discrimination (article 2). Children were right in that a real wolf would constitute a danger for children if he went to school with them but they showed inability to understand that Wilson was an imaginary character and that the author did not intend to write a horror story about real wolves in school with people. This, however, could be encouraging, because the girls asked for segregation based on concerns for children's safety and on facts and not on stereotypes and prejudice. These children's fears imply the need for the school for Wilson to provide for children's right to protection from physical violence (article 19) and even children right to life (article 6).

Social Environment

Children also answered my question about the teacher in the perfect school for Wilson. The teacher would give him and the other wolves food and teach them about the frailty of human bodies and not eating them.

ES: And what will the teacher do?

She will give them [wolves] sweets to eat.

She'd better give them meat to eat because wolves eat only meat.

ES: Sweets and meat [for the wolves], then. And the teacher. Apart from giving them food, what else should the teacher do?

She will teach them.

ES: What else will the teacher do apart from feeding them?

They will have lessons to teach them how human beings are, that they have bones and teach them not to eat people.

But these wolves do not eat people.

This group was afraid of the safety of children (article 19) if they shared a school with wolves. Their fear of wolves at school was such that all they could talk about was teachers protecting children from harm by wolves. They are the same children who in their first session were too afraid for children safety from parties other than their teachers and peers (see Chapter 6).

Elm School MX1

None of the children in this group was in a session in which the plan for the traditional school was discussed. They participated in sessions where the plans for a school based on traditional developmental psychology and a rights-based school were discussed. Children in this group described their school as a perfect school for Wilson and added further features they would want his school to have. These were toys and equipment for play and learning indoors (*e.g.* computers, chairs), unhealthy food and a classroom layout like the one of their own classroom (*e.g.* with play corners and a circle time area). They did not discuss the teacher's role and the only thing they said that resembled a rule was that children should be polite to each other.

Physical Environment

The following excerpt refers to toys and other resources as well as acceptable activities and behaviors among children in the perfect school for Wilson.

ES: What kind of school would Wilson like?

One like the one we have now.

ES: How is the one you have now like, then?

Our school is full of toys.

ES: So, he would like a school with many toys.

And full of chairs and benches.

And he would like us [himself and this group children] having sweets.

We could all be together in school and in the classrooms and could all be polite.

ES: What else would make him want to go to school?

I like food.

ES: So, [he would like] that you eat together?

Nods yes.

If we had a television he could have enjoyed it.

If they [in the perfect school for Wilson] had a computer, we could play DVDs all the time.

Ours is broken.

ES: What else do you think he would have liked?

A large yard where we can play together every day.

But we have a slope in our yard and it feels like an uphill when we go up and a downhill when we go down. And it is straight and has a turn and it used to have railings and so it looked like a snake yard.

ES: So you are saying that Wilson would like a yard that would have an uphill slope?

It would have downhill slopes and plenty of toys and equipment.

ES: Like what?

Slides, see saws, jungle bars.

And a winding slide.

I like such slides.

And it would have bicycles for all and skateboards.

Ma'am[6], I have been to a playground and it had two slides.

ES: So, should it (the ideal yard for Wilson) have two slides? One like this (straight) and one like that (winding)?

I prefer long straight slides.

I like winding ones.

ES: So, what would the school look like from the inside to make him want to attend?

It can have a television, toys, a lot of space, lots and lots of toys.

ES: Toys like what?

And a whole carpet for the circle time area for eighteen children.

It would have a puppet theatre.

It will have a carpet, a number line ...

It will have plenty of toys, Lego, toy kitchen and a puppet theatre.

And a bookcase.

And a toy green grocer's (corner / play area).

We will have a basketball court and a football playground.

In terms of the physical environment of the school, they suggested a spacious schoolyard and resources but not time to play. Their answers indicate that their right to play (article 31) was important to them and wanted Wilson to enjoy it, too. Furthermore, they linked their right to play to their right to freedom of association (article 15).

Children wanted to play and eat together with their peers and Wilson and to be polite to each other. These comments also reflect the importance of company and even friendship and indirectly appropriate behavior rules related to article 29(d) of the Convention, that is, an education preparing them to live with understanding, peace, tolerance, equality for sexes and friendship with peoples. They did not discuss the role of an early years teacher or the rules of acceptable behavior in school further, so there is no section on the social environment of the perfect school for Wilson.

Oak School AU

Children in this group did not mention any specific play equipment or resources in the schoolyard; they were vague by saying toys were necessary for the perfect school for Wilson. They believed that little pigeons would be a necessary feature of the perfect school for Wilson as well as Wilson having friends.

The Physical Environment

Apart from the play resources this group mentioned, they also asked for resources, such as books, paints and tables. Depending on who uses these resources, they can be work-related or related to play indoors, that is, used both for teacher-directed activities as well as child-initiated activities according to Wood (2010).

ES: What school would make Wilson want to go to it?

[A school] With toys.

With food.

With books.

With paintings.

With friends.

ES: What else?

With little tables.

ES: Any other idea for the kindergarten for Wilson?

To have carpets.

To have toys.

To have puzzles.

To have little pigeons.

Children did not make comments about the space and time allocated to play in the school for Wilson. Children views reflect the priority they gave to their right to play (article 31) and to nutrition (article 24) in imagining the perfect school for Wilson. The implementation of article 15 about children's right of freedom of association can be facilitated by having and making friends in school, which the children suggested.

Some of the resources (*e.g.* books) children mentioned can be used in tasks assigned to children by their teachers or they can be used in tasks children themselves organize. It has been recorded that children tend to consider the activities they choose themselves as games / play and the activities their teachers give them as work, even though they may be teacher-organized play or playful activities (Howard, 2010; Wood, 2010). Books, for instance, can be considered play or a child initiated activity when children choose to read, whereas it is work when the teacher reads to them or ask them to read. Therefore, these views are related to children's right to education, which develops their personality and abilities in a child-friendly and child-centered way (article 29(a) and GC 7 2005) as well as their right to play (article 31).

The Social Environment

According to the children, the teacher's work and classroom rules were inextricably bound up. The teacher was not to scold the children and Wilson when they broke the rules but the only rule about unacceptable behavior clearly stated by the children was not hitting others. However, this was soon changed into '*not be beaten*' by other children or the teacher. This change in their utterances from active to passive voice could mean that their emphasis on this rule was not exclusively because they appreciated peaceful coexistence with classmates but because they wanted protection from physical abuse. This need for protection extends to their teachers, too, as the children claimed they would not have tolerated such a behavior (*i.e.* hitting) from their teacher.

ES: What should the teacher be like so that he wants to go?

Good.

ES: What do you mean when you say good?

Not to tell us off a lot.

ES: What rules should this class have to make Wilson want to go?

Not to hit others.

Not to have bad children.

ES: What else should the perfect for Wilson school have?

To learn the shapes.

Not to be beaten.

Yes, because in the old days, they used to grab a stick and beat.

ES: *The teachers? So, it wouldn't be nice for the teacher to hit you, eh?*

If the teacher hits me, I will leave this school and never come back.

Me, too.

Children's right to protection from physical harm (article 19) was prioritized as well as the teacher not criticizing them angrily when they misbehave. The latter is relevant to article 28.2 of the Convention which recommends respect toward children's dignity when disciplining them at school. These children must have often resorted to physical violence when disagreeing whereas their teachers to scolding and shouting at them. Teachers observed the law and article 19 of the Convention but not children themselves. The observation of article 19 was very significant to their idea of a school for Wilson.

Oak School DP

Children from Oak School mainly discussed the resources of the school and the perfect teacher for Wilson.

Physical Environment

These children referred to resources both for play indoors (*e.g.* puzzles) and outdoors (*e.g.* slides) and for children learning (*e.g.* worksheets). Animals in the schoolyard were also desirable.

ES: *What should a school be like so that Wilson will want to go?*

To have little tables.

To have paper to draw on.

To have many friends.

To have puzzles.

To have a yard.

To have a slide.

To have swings.

A see saw.

To have legos.

Computer games.

PlayStation.

ES: What should the yard have?

Butterflies.

Clowns to make us laugh.

Treasure hunt.

To have a swimming pool.

To have a little pond.

Waterslides.

To have horses.

To have a toy Spiderman.

A dog.

And ducks.

And kittens.

Trees.

To have flying dinosaurs

ES: What do you mean?

Balloons (in the form of dinosaurs).

Contact with nature was essential to this perfect school for Wilson. Children talked about a schoolyard with trees, horses, dogs, ducks and kittens. Paragraph e of article 29 was to be facilitated in the school for Wilson, as they wanted fauna and flora. This discussion shows that children emphasized both their right to play (article 31) as well as their right to education (articles 28-29) as necessary elements of the perfect school for Wilson.

Social Environment

Children in this group wanted a more encouraging teacher who would praise their work and Wilson's, which is in accordance with a child-friendly and child-centered education (article 28 of GC 7 2005).

ES: What else should the school have?

A teacher that is good.

ES: What is a good teacher like?

Says to the children who do nice works "Well done, nice work, you draw really well".

To have trees as well.

To have worksheets.

And shapes.

To learn about numbers.

To learn to read.

All the play resources these children considered necessary in relation to worksheets and learning the basics show that these children did not devalue learning (articles 28.1 and 29(a)) as it is offered in their school but that perhaps they thought Wilson and young children needed more play (article 31). Having good friends would be good for Wilson as well as a supporting and encouraging teacher as compared to what they were experiencing.

Oak School RB

The physical environment for the perfect school for Wilson had to have both play and learning resources.

Physical Environment

These children's answers exhibited consideration for Wilson's habits described in the book and they were related to the group's own experience of schooling. So, combined, they mentioned he should be allowed to watch television and rest, while at school but they also added the necessity for him to learn the basics so as to be prepared for primary school. The rest of their suggestions for the perfect school for Wilson were about resources for play.

ES: What kindergarten do you think would make Wilson want to go to it?

One where he can sleep and watch television.

ES: So only a school where there would be a television set and a bed?

I do the same thing. I sleep late and want to watch children's programs in the morning.

You need to learn reading and writing or you will not go to primary school.

Babies do not go!

ES: So, how would it [a school] be so that Wilson would want to go?

It should have a swing.

Flowers.

Slides.

See saw.

Monkey bars.

Boxing sack.

ES: What would the classroom have so that he would want to enter?

Circle time area.

Toys.

Benches.

ES: Any ideas?

It should have a trampoline.

And an inflatable.

An indoors natatorium.

A swimming pool to learn to swim.

Balloons.

ES: Anything else?

To have [materials for] painting.

And drawers.

Tables on which to draw.

Cupboards.

A little later, they expanded more on resources.

It should have legos.

ES: Anything else?

Plasticine.

And the tools for plasticine.

And boxes.

It should have markers and glitters.

And computers.

And tablets.

And backgammon and chess.

Board games.

Snakes and ladders, Ludo and guess who?.

These views indicate that respecting children's right to play and leisure (article 31) and to education (articles 28.1-29(a)) were basic features of the perfect school for Wilson.

Social Environment

The children discussed the best teacher and the rules for the perfect school for Wilson. This teacher would read Wilson and his classmates stories and use videos, perhaps to teach them something or for entertainment. Entertainment seems more likely as an explanation because this suggestion was complimented with music and dancing, which the teacher would allow them.

ES: And what is the teacher supposed to do in the class to make Wilson want to come in?

To show them videos.

To play music for them.

To let them dance.

To read them stories.

The rules children considered necessary for the perfect school for Wilson regarded their own physical safety (*e.g.* no beating, no hitting, no speeding) and the safety of everybody's property. The teacher, however, was not supposed to be strict about the implementation of rules by the children in the school perfect for Wilson.

ES: And what rules must this class have to make him want to go?

To go slower[7].

The teacher should not be strict.

ES: So, not to have a strict teacher. What rules should they have?

Not to beat others, not to hit each other,

Not to break other people's crosses because they are God's and we should be careful.

In terms of the social environment of the perfect school for Wilson, children's right to play and leisure (article 31) was emphasized. Safety and protection from physical harm (article 19) were reflected in their views of classroom rules. A teacher who was not harsh and unyielding, when it came to rules was desirable and in accordance with GC 1 2001 and GC 7 2005 for a child friendly approach to children's education.

Pine School AU

The physical environment of the perfect school for Wilson was to be full of play resources, entertainment resources and music.

Physical Environment

Wilson's habit of watching television a lot was taken into consideration and children from Pine School wanted a TV set included in the best school for Wilson. They would add toys (*e.g.* tablets, toy fish) as well as musical instruments. Contact and play with water in the form of swimming pools and water slides were also mentioned. These children thought that making friends in school is an incentive for Wilson to attend school.

ES: What should the kindergarten have to make him (Wilson) want to go [to school]?

Toys.

A television.

To be close [to his home].

To go out to the yard whenever his likes.

To be allowed to look through the teacher's stuff.

To play with a tablet or a mobile.

To have a piano and a lyre.

Yes, and a toy that I like very much. It has some fish that open their mouths and three fishing rods and you try to catch them.

I would like a fish which we can squeeze to make it drink water.

ES: A real one?

No, a toy.

ES: Other toys for the yard of the perfect [for Wilson] school? What would it have?

A swimming pool.

Sea.

A ladder [to reach the diving board].

ES: What do you mean it would have sea?

To be close to the sea.

ES: What else?

Waterslides.

Tents.

And a see saw. But not close to the gravels.

[I want] the waterslides to lead to the pool and to also have a little door so that we can go into the sea.

I would want it to have boxes outside where children could hide and their mothers would not be able to find them.

And their teacher [would not be able to find them].

And then they would open their doors (of the boxes), get out of the boxes and leave.

ES: Any other ideas to make Wilson want to go to school?

To give him a canvas to paint on.

To make many friends.

These children really appreciated children's right to play and leisure (article 31) and wanted it to be respected in the school for Wilson. They also requested contact with nature while at school, which implies that an education cultivating respect for the environment was likely to be facilitated in the school for Wilson (article 29).

The Social Environment

These children did not like cleaning after themselves or a teacher that forces them to do so for Wilson. They would love a teacher who lets Wilson go out in the yard twice each morning session[8] and does not punish him for breaking the rules, particularly since this group mentioned that children should be allowed to go through their teacher's stuff. The ideal teacher should also not shout at Wilson and give him nice things she makes.

ES: Well, let me ask you something else. Who would be a perfect teacher for Wilson so that he would want to go to school?

Mrs X.

Mrs Y.

Mrs Z.[9]

ES: Will you tell me what these teachers did that was so perfect?

Our teacher put scotch tape on the floor and we shouldn't go beyond it or we would lose!

ES: Ah, she showed you nice games! So, the perfect teacher organizes nice games. What else?

She allows them (children) to go out twice (a day).

They (the perfect teachers) do not tell children off.

She makes nice things and gives them to children.

She does not make children clean the classroom.

She does not shout at us.

She does not punish us.

ES: Even if you damage things?

Yes, even when we do not listen to them (teachers).

This group was they only one who wanted more time for Wilson in the yard. When describing the perfect school for him the importance of play (article 31) for a school for Wilson was raised. Children were too curious (seeing what the teacher brings before she shows it to them), too playful (being allowed to go out or hide for their teacher and parents to find) and not so responsible (not cleaning after themselves) perhaps in ways their teachers did not appreciate. This indicates that they had not learned some of the acceptable behaviors relevant to their responsibilities in school and the structure and the operation of a kindergarten. Of course, that does not mean that it is the children fault, since their parents and their teachers are also parties interested in education, among others. Children believed that punishments and scolding were not desirable, a topic already discussed in Chapter 4, whereas nice things as presents from adults were desirable. This reluctance and resistance to being responsible for oneself agrees with what children in Scotland said about the need for a robot or a servant already discussed earlier in this chapter.

Pine School MX

Children in this group, like the group from Elm School, considered play equipment and toys as the most important thing for a school perfect for Wilson, as they talked about them for most of the session.

Physical Environment

The answers of this group were influenced by the children's own school layout and daily routine, as were those from Elm School. They talked about the pupil's equipment and signing in the attendance book in the morning. However, children and Wilson eating unhealthy food together at tea time was not part of their routine but they considered it necessary for the perfect school for Wilson.

ES: What would he liked in a school to make him want to go?

To play.

ES: To have the opportunity to play. And to play what?

The same games we play.

ES: *What games do you play?*

Toy cars.

And a toy kitchen and tinkering things and toy animals.

A toy shop.

ES: *What do you think that the school should have to make Wilson want to go?*

He would take his bag with snacks and water and in the morning he would write his name[10] and play in the corners.

Like we write it (their name) in the attendance book every morning.

ES: *Would this school have a yard? Would he like it to have a yard?*

Yes.

ES: *And what would this yard have?*

A Slide.

A slide, a swing, it should have a brown and a white one and monkey bars.

A play house.

Furthermore, they expanded on resources that their own school did not provide, such as having animals both domesticated and wild, *i.e.* a horse, a dog, a duckling, little birds and a lion, in the school yard. They seemed to care about the animal's welfare, because they wanted to build jumping obstacles and stables for their horses and a jungle for their little lion.

ES: *(And what would this yard have?) What do you think?*

A horse.

To have [a school that offers] horse riding there.

ES: *Ah, have real horses so that they can go riding?*

Yes, I have done horse riding in Thessaloniki.[11]

I have done horse riding in Fun Fair.[12]

ES: Would the horse be in the school yard or somewhere near the kindergarten? What are your thoughts?

In the middle as we walk inwards.

ES: In the school yard?

Yes.

ES: So a large yard to fit the horses? Would it have stables?

Yes.

They would also have obstacles so that the horses can jump and children can have fun.

ES: And who would take care of the horses?

We would.

A farmer.

ES: And why not you, like Anne said?

Because we will have classes and will not be able to take care of them all the time.

ES: And when you can? When you have free time, will you take care of your little horses?

We have [free time].

Food.

ES: So, you will feed them?

Yes.

We will take them for walks in the yard.

And it would have little hens, too.

And a rope.

And a duckling.

ES: A skipping rope for children to play?

Yes.

And a puppy.

ES: A dog puppy?

Yes.

And a little lion.

ES: Where would you keep the little lion?

In a cage.

ES: Would you let it walk around?

We will let it. If it does not hurt others ...

We will train it.

ES: Will you train it?

Yes.

Yes, together with the farmer who will be helping us.

So that it doesn't bite us.

Farmers do not have lions.

We will build a jungle as well.

ES: Should we bring in a grown-up who knows about lions? To take care of your little lion?

Yes, and we will have a leash for it.

ES: Do you have any other ideas that would make the school attractive so that Wilson would want to go?

Yes, I know.

To have a decorated classroom.

To have a pool.

ES: What should the classroom have?

Ribbons.

Little flags.

Umbrellas.

A little later, while they were discussing the social environment of the perfect school for Wilson, they made more comments on the physical environment.

It should also have toys and a gym in the yard.

And flowers and plants.

And seats in the yard for children to rest.

ES: And some of them indoors?

Yes and little mattresses.

ES: And you, Nelly, what were you saying?

And a refrigerator outside as well.

To put food, whatever we want to eat. To put cakes in it.

Cup cakes, sandwiches, cakes and let it[13] (Wilson) have turkey.

To have a tree that makes meat!

And ice cubes.

ES: Any other ideas?

And ice-cream.

An ice cream van.

Little birds.

To have mattresses in other classrooms and for children to come together and sleep.

The above mean that children's right to play (article 31) was important enough to these children so as to form the most important part of the perfect school for Wilson. All their ideas about a school where animals are kept and children are allowed to participate in animal care show how easy it would be for a teacher to implement article 29(e) about an education cultivating respect for the environment. These children realized that they would need help from an adult to take care of the animals, which indicates that they were aware of their need to be taught and shown how to do certain things. So, in a way, their right to education was further confirmed as necessary for the perfect school for Wilson. This is also an indication that these children knew that they were not equal to expert adults such as a farmer or a lion tamer but confident that they could learn from them and master the skills of these experts.

Social Environment

Children discussed behaviors in school, which indirectly is a topic related to rules, and then they continued to talk about the yard of the perfect school for Wilson. However, their first comment was about Wilson's and his peers' behavior. They wanted a calm environment and a teacher who is strict to children breaking the rules, which provides this calmness. Simultaneously, they wanted Wilson to be able to do whatever he wants at school. When asked what if he wanted to beat other children, they mentioned rules about their safety.

This group of children seemed to ask for more freedom, just like the group from Elm School. However, they did not link this freedom to some of their classroom rules, which protect them from others being allowed to do whatever they want to them. They appreciated being safe and having rules to be protected, which seemed to be the only infringement of their freedom that they desired. They wanted more autonomy in other aspects of their school life, however.

ES: What should the kindergarten be like to make Wilson want to go there?

[It should be] calm.

The teacher to be strict when children do silly things.

Children went on to describe the physical environment further so a little later I asked:

ES: Any other ideas about how to make him want to go to school?

[Wilson will be allowed] to do what he wants.

ES: So, what if he wants to beat you?

Eeee ... (a shriek showing that they do not like the idea)

ES: Can we do whatever we want?

Only during the breaks.

And if he has a knife?

Maybe he will run after us to hit us with a stick.

Children appreciated their right to leisure, rest and play (article 31). They were interested not only in flora but in fauna in the schoolyard, which forms a strong basis for the successful implementation of article 29(e). They, too, mentioned food, both unhealthy and partly healthy for people and with consideration for Wilson and his being a carnivore. They wanted a calm atmosphere in school and were the only group who wanted a teacher strict with children 'behaving silly', that is, children who break the rules regarding their protection from physical harm. Being able to do what they wanted and decide themselves was allowed to these children only during breaks, that is, when children go to the yard and choose what to do or play, and that was extended to Wilson. Their words were too general and vague (do whatever they and Wilson want), whereas they seemed to appreciate compromising some of their freedom for the safety it procures.

The last comment about children's sleepovers in school indicates that they wanted the company of their peers in other classes and not only of their classmates. This is in accordance with article 15 and children's freedom of association. Furthermore, it indicates that some children feel they do not have enough time with other children in school to do stuff together, which is a particularly important aspect of their education (Li, 2022) since they attend a kindergarten and not a primary school. This is related to article 29(d) and to the grounds of cultivating a spirit of peace, tolerance, equality of sexes and friendship among all peoples as not all children in school have the same culture. It is also relevant to article 6(c) of the GC 7 2005, which explains that young children learn to negotiate and coordinate shared activities, resolve conflicts, keep agreements and accept responsibility for others through their relationships with other children. At the same time it indicates that for some children their education is not as child-friendly and child-centered as defined by articles 11(b), 14(c), 23, 28 and 34 of GC 7 2005 and as they would like and probably need it to be.

Comparison of Data Within Greece

In this section of the chapter, the findings regarding the discussion on the excerpt from the book *Whiffy Wilson, the wolf who wouldn't go to school* are analyzed. Eight focus group sessions took place with children from Greece. All groups described a school with plenty of play resources, two of them (Elm MX and Pine MX) required ample space for play and one group (Pine AU) more time for play outdoors.

Nature was as important for the school for Wilson. Fauna was desirable in the school for Wilson according to half of the groups (Elm AU, Oak AU, Oak DP and Pine MX) and flora according to three groups (Oak DP, Oak RB, and Pine MX). Sweets and other foods, healthy or not, were mentioned by half of the groups (Elm RB, Elm MX, Oak AU and Pine MX) and only children from Oak AU did not mention sweets.

References to learning were made only by the children participating in the groups from Oak School (Oak AU, Oak DP and Oak RB). They mainly mentioned the 3R's and to a lesser extent they referred to filling in worksheets, watching videos, being read stories (Oak RB). Children in Elm RB talked about the need for wolves, like Wilson, being taught about human biology and how to avoid eating humans.

As for the social environment, friendships with other children were important to children mainly from Oak School (Oak AU, Oak DP, and Elm MX). The teacher whom Wilson needs was not perceived in the same way by all groups in Greece. According to those who referred to the perfect teacher for Wilson, she should be one not shouting at children (Elm AU, Oak AU and Pine AU), when they break the rules, she should be encouraging children, when they are doing well (Oak DP), making them happy (Elm AU) and enriching children's play and making them gifts (Pine AU). A strict teacher who expects everybody to follow the rules and punishes disobedience was desirable only by children in Pine MX.

In terms of classroom rules, the most popular ones were these referring to children being protected from physical harm by other people (Elm AU, Oak AU and Oak RB). Rules about taking care of the physical environment were mentioned only by children from Elm AU, whereas children's from Pine AU did not wish any rules in the perfect school for Wilson.

Even though the children from Greece attended kindergarten and were not officially required to learn academic subjects in an academic way, they took it for granted that play was the most important feature of a school perfect for Wilson and they mainly spoke about aspects of play. The low score of indulgence which characterizes Greece restrained children who wanted more of their wish to play to be satisfied. The power distance between children and their teachers may also have contributed to children complaining about strict rules and strict teachers shouting at children. Learning was not excluded and friendships with peers were also significant. The high score of collectivism in Greece may have something to do with the importance children gave to being and doing things together with other children in school.

Comparison of Data From Scotland And Greece

When comparing the findings of the second focus group sessions with children from Greece and Scotland, all groups but one in Scotland (Valley MX1) made comments about the necessity of play resources for the perfect school for Wilson, thus about children's and Wilson's right to play (article 31). In terms of time for play, half of the groups in Scotland suggested more time for play (Valley MX2 and Hill DP) and only one out of eight groups in Greece (Pine AU). This means that children in Scotland felt a more urgent need for play in school, which could be due to the difference between attending a primary school rather than a kindergarten. Furthermore, only children in Greece requested more space for play, a large yard in particular (Elm MX and Pine MX) for the perfect school for Wilson. This could be because of the less financial attention Greece pays to its schools as compared to Scotland.

When it comes to flora and fauna in the schoolyard, half of the groups of children in Scotland (Valley MX2 and Hill AU) mentioned flora only. On the other hand, in Greece nearly half of the groups talked about the significance of flora (Oak DP, Oak RB and Pine MX) and half of the groups about the significance of fauna (Elm AU, Oak AU, Oak DP, and Pine MX) for the perfect school for Wilson. Children's ideas suggest that the implementation of article 29(e) could be facilitated in these classes but there is an interest in a wider range of natural environments in Greece.

Sweets were very popular with the groups in Scotland as three out of the four groups mentioned them (Valley MX2, Hill AU, and Hill DP) as necessary for the perfect school for Wilson. On the contrary, children in Greece mentioned them to a lesser extent, three groups out of eight (Elm RB, Elm MX, and Oak RB). There was only one group (Oak AU) who mentioned food in general, rather than something unhealthy for the school for Wilson. Therefore most of the children in both countries who referred to food in the perfect school for Wilson, were not in favor of the implementation of article 24 of the Convention, which refers to children's right to healthy nutrition.

As for learning at the perfect school for Wilson, views were split in Scotland with half of the groups (Valley MX1 and Hill AU) wanting lessons (*e.g.* the 3 R's) to take place in the school and the other half not wanting any work assigned to Wilson and his classmates by their teacher (Valley MX2 and Hill DP). Children in Scotland who did not wish lessons for Wilson also mentioned the need for a robot (Hill DP) and a servant (Valley MX2) to help him with his work at school. There is a correspondence between learning and pupil's equipment only for the group from Scotland (Valley MX1). The above implies that there was something about the teaching methodology or the number of activities that children had to participate in that was not welcome by half of the groups of children and that they did not want Wilson to experience it. Apart from the structure of the primary school in Scotland, the high score of indulgence in the country may explain children's answers.

In Greece, nearly half (three out of eight) of the groups (all three groups from Oak School) considered learning as an essential part of the perfect school for Wilson, while the rest did not mention anything relevant to learning.

A few children in both countries talked about the equipment of a pupil, Valley MX1 in Scotland and Pine MX in Greece. However, these two groups did not agree on learning at school; children in Valley MX1 would add lessons to the perfect school for Wilson, whereas, children in Pine MX did not include them.

As for the social environment of the perfect school for Wilson, children in the two countries had different ideas about the perfect teacher for Wilson in relation to rule making. Children in Hill DP wanted a teacher who would do, and allow children to do, *crazy* things, whereas children in Valley MX1 described the teacher as somebody *nice*. This group used the word nice to describe the rules (*e.g.* play nicely), too, borrowing the term from the rules in their own school.

Even though children in Greece did not describe the teacher or her rules as *crazy* and *silly* like children in Scotland did, they, too, wanted a more lax atmosphere in school with teachers allowing children to break the rules or not shouting at them when they do break the rules (Elm AU, Oak AU, and Pine AU). Some of the children in Greece related the teacher's role with the happiness of children (Elm AU), their encouragement (Oak DP) and their play (Pine AU). Only children from

Pine MX group wanted a strict teacher, who does not allow children to violate the classroom rules.

A teacher was not considered necessary in the school for Wilson by only one group in Scotland (Hill AU) and in Greece, only children in Elm RB mentioned biology as a subject for the teacher to teach in the perfect school for Wilson.

Children in Scotland wanted Wilson to participate in rule-making (Hill AU) whereas children in Hill DP mentioned the class having crazy rules, that is, definitively not rules that adults traditionally want in school. Some children in Greece referred to rules about Wilson's and his classmates' protection from physical harm by others (Elm AU, Oak AU, and Oak RB) and only children in Elm AU and Pine AU mentioned rules about tidiness in the classroom. It is evident that, even though children in Scotland and Greece gave different emphasis on aspects of rules and rule-making in school, rules and the process by which they were set in both countries were not favored. This means that there is scope for the better or proper implementation of article 12 in both countries, when it comes to defining what the appropriate behavior for young children in school should be.

A final difference between the countries was that only children in Greece (Oak AU and Oak DP) mentioned the importance of being friends with classmates in the perfect school for Wilson. These children's idea of friendship among classmates is in line with article 6(c) of the GC 7 2005. Children from Valley MX1 groups in Scotland mentioned children's sharing and being nice to one another, which has some relevance to the relationship among peers. Both views seem to facilitate article 29(d), on children's preparation for responsible adult life in schools and in a broader sense article 15 on children's right to freedom of association. However, the views of children in Greece on friendships may be due to the higher score of collectivism characterizing Greece according to Hofstede (2021b) as compared to Scotland.

NOTES

[1] I used pseudonyms because I wanted to clarify that a boy and a girl spoke and had different opinions.

[2] All of the participants in this group were girls.

[3] Star time is the pseudonym I used in the chapter dedicated to the school based on developmental psychology.

[4] A pseudonym for their teacher's name to ensure everybody's anonymity.

[5] In Greek the expression the girl used is emphatic and used to accentuate difference. *Ένα είναι τα ζωάκια, ένα είναι τα παιδάκια.*

[6] Some children did call me Eva (as I asked them and the teachers in both countries to call me) but some of them called me ma'am. In Greece it is respectful but not distant to call a teacher ma'am or sir whereas in Scotland the respectful thing would be to call them Mr Somebody or Mrs Somebody. Children never called me Mrs Synodi, although nobody introduced me like that, especially in Scotland.

[7] Wolves are faster than children, so Wilson must be careful with his speed.

[8] Morning sessions only were compulsory for all children in Greece at that time.

[9] They mentioned the names of teachers in Pine school.

[10] Every morning children in kindergarten sign the class register.

[11] I left the name of the city the child mentioned because the sample did not come from that place in Greece.

[12] I have used a pseudonym (Fun Fair) because the child told us the name of the facility, which was relatively close to the place where this particular group came from.

[13] In the sessions, the children and consequently I used the expression little wolf. In Greek 'little wolf' is neuter in gender, even though they knew it was a little male wolf.

CHAPTER 8

Conclusions

Abstract: In this chapter, the topic of this study is described, together with its importance for the education of young children. The methodological approach to this research is also examined as well as its main findings. It attempts to give voice to children from Greece and Scotland aged 5 to 6 years about the education of children their age. Children's views underlined the significance of their right to play (article 31) and their right to participate in decision-making (article 12). At the end of the chapter, the implications of this study are considered together with further topics of investigation relevant to children's rights in school. It is concluded that more initiatives need to be taken regarding the implementation of article 5 of the Convention, which pertains to the adults' role in helping children exercise their rights.

Keywords: Children's rights, Children's right to play, Comparative Education, Education, Focus groups, Participation, Qualitative research, Safety, Young children.

INTRODUCTION

The aim of this book was to give voice to children, aged 5 to 6 years, regarding the education of children their age and then relate these voices to children's rights as defined in the Convention of the Rights of the Child (1989). More specifically, the purpose of this study was to explore five-year-old children's views on aspects of behavior and rules, learning and play, and the physical environment of a school and to relate these views to the implementation or not of various provision, protection and participation rights (Te One, 2011) that children are entitled to and pertain to school. In this study, the term voice was used as Jones and Welch (2018) defined it rather than as related to children agency and participation determined by childhood studies (Lee 1998). I employed the term *voice* because many children are still 'silenced, not listened to or have adults speak for them' (Jones & Welch, 2018, p. 118) when decisions affecting them are made.

The topic of giving children an opportunity to voice their ideas on the education of young children was considered significant, because there is a tendency for many people to ignore or underestimate children's views due to their young age rather than their inability to form opinions and think rationally. That definitely deprives children of their right to be consulted and their opinions to be listened to and be seriously considered when decisions are made affecting children's lives (article 12 of the Convention). Another reason this research is significant is its comparative nature, since there are not many studies comparing the opinions of children from different countries on aspects of different schooling.

Methodology of Research

As for the methodological approach to this empirical research, it was comparative and qualitative. Children views on aspects of schooling were produced in two countries, Scotland and Greece. The significance of comparison is that it leads to a deeper understanding of education phenomena and the impact of societal factors (*e.g.* economy, governance, politics, culture) on them (Calogiannaki, 2011; Clarkson, 2009; Georgeson *et al.*, 2013; Kazamias, 2009; Lubeck, 1995; Phillips & Schweisfurth, 2011).

The education for children aged five years in Scotland and Greece was selected for various reasons so as to enable the research to be viable, productive, worthwhile and manageable (Clarkson, 2009). Scotland and Greece were chosen because of their difference in economic affluence and what it entails for their education systems. Scotland was selected because it is considered a rich country, whereas Greece is struggling to survive. The difference in affluence means that there is less financial aid to education in Greece as compared to Scotland, which entails less choices for children and limited scope for participation in decision-making for the children as well as the teachers.

Scotland and Greece were also selected because of three particular differences in their national cultures (Hofstede, 2021a). The three cultural dimensions between Greece and the United Kingdom [part of which is Scotland], as defined and measured by Hofstede that were relevant to the topic of children's education and their rights are (a) power distance (Hofstede, 2019a), (b) indulgence (Hofstede, 2019b) and (c) individualism (Hofstede, 2021b). The score on power distance is higher for Greece (Hofstede, 2019a); it is almost double compared with that of the UK (60 versus 35). On the contrary, in terms of individualism, UK scores 91 as compared to 35 for Greece, almost three times higher than Greece. As for indulgence, the UK scores higher (Hofstede, 2019b) than Greece (69 versus 50) but the difference between the countries is not as sharp as with the aforementioned dimensions.

These differences may have manifested in the form of children expecting or even receiving more adult directed education from their teachers in Greece and thus children's scope for consultation or participation in school being narrower as compared to that of Scotland. However, each person has their own culture, that is, their own way to 'relate to other people, to think, to behave and their own worldview' (Rodriguez, 1999, as cited in Samovar *et al.*, 2013, p. 35). This means that not all the dimensions of one's national culture are accepted by people and this applies to teachers as well as pupils (Keesing, 1974). Therefore, depending on their national culture, the culture of the school children attend, their teacher's culture, and their own culture, children may have had different perceptions of the best school provision for them.

Simultaneously, Greece and Scotland had similarities which justified their selection for comparison. They are both located in Europe, were both part of the European Union when the empirical research in Scotland took place and are countries with mainly a Christian population and past (Report on International Religious Freedom: United Kingdom, 2017; Report on International Religious Freedom: Greece, 2017). Therefore, over the centuries, people in Scotland and Greece have known aspects of similar cultures, philosophies and ideas about educating young children.

Child-centeredness in education is considered a means of facilitating the implementation of young children's rights (General Comment 7 2005, articles 14, 17, 23, 28, and 34) and it exists in some form in the official education provision of both countries. Five year old children in Scotland attend primary school for the first time, but Scotland has at least two decades of child-centered primary education starting in 1965 (Darling, 2004) more than Greece. Their peers in Greece attend kindergartens, therefore, more time for play is allowed to them as compared to children in Scotland.

The final reason for choosing Scotland and Greece was practical. Since data were to be produced using an oral method of investigation, focus groups, and I am a native Greek speaker fluent in English, these two countries were within my options. Such a choice also enabled me to ensure linguistic equivalence, which should characterize every comparative study (Broadfoot, Osborn, with Gilly, & Bûcher, 1993).

The data for this comparison was chosen to be produced qualitatively. Each child participated in two focus group sessions (Flick, 2007; Gibson, 2007; Kitzinger, 1994; Large & Beheshti, 2001). In the first one, they discussed one of three plans for a school for children of their age. These plans were for a teacher-directed school, for a school based on developmental psychology and for a rights-based school. These three models of school reflect different degrees of respect towards children's rights, with the teacher directed model showing respect to a minimum number of rights and a rights-based model showing respect to all rights. Children were asked to suggest improvements for the plan they were read, so that they could be given to the queen and king who were considering the plans for implementation in their country.

In the second session, children were read the beginning of the book *Whiffy Wilson, the wolf who wouldn't go to school* (Hart, 2014). Then they were asked to describe the school that would make Wilson want to attend.

The research questions attempted to be answered were:

1. Which aspects of the school plans presented to them are children in favor of? Which rights do they refer to?
2. Which aspects of the school plans presented to them are children not in favor of? Which rights do they refer to?
3. Which particular aspects of school provision and practices do children prioritize and include when imagining the best school for Wilson and by default for young children? Which rights do the children's views reflect?
4. Are children's views similar or different across countries? On which aspects of schooling? For what possible reason?
5. Are children's views similar or different within a country? On which aspects of schooling? For what possible reason?

Questions 1 and 2 were answered by data from the first focus group session and question 3 was answered by data from the second focus group session. Questions 4 and 5 were answered by data from both sessions.

Main Findings of the First Focus Group Sessions

The Physical Environment of a School and Children's Rights

As for the physical environment of the best school ever, findings from all focus group sessions in both countries indicated that children prioritized their right to play and leisure (article 31). Regardless of the plan for a school read to them, all children wanted more play resources and equipment mainly for the school yard. The fact that they related their play to the school yard reinforces the thesis that children tend to consider activities that they themselves initiate as play (Howard, 2010; Wood, 2010), even though their teachers may be initiating games for them to play. A division between the teachers' realm, which is the classroom and the children's realm, which is the schoolyard became evident. However, some of the resources children considered as missing from the plans, such as a library and its books, were resources which can be used both for teacher initiated and children initiated activities. This means that children did not reject the idea of being educated (articles 28 and 29) in school as well as play.

Some children who discussed the plan for a teacher directed school also made comments about the time and space for play in the best school. Children in Valley School in Scotland wanted a larger playground and more time for play, whereas in Greece children from Pine School wanted more space both indoors and outdoors but did not mention anything relevant to time for play.

Only children from Hill School who were read the plan for a school based on developmental psychology, discussed the need for more space for play. None of the respective focus groups in Greece made any comments relevant to space and time dedicated to play and child initiated activities.

Children in Valley School, Scotland who were read the plan for a rights-based school thought that the time dedicated to play was too much, misinterpreting the plan, which mentioned that children's play would not be interrupted by teachers. They also seemed to have misinterpreted the many resources described in the plan as play resources only, even though they could be used for teacher led activities (*e.g.* books). None of the children from the three focus groups in Greece read the rights-based plan for a school made any comments on time and space for play.

Contact with animals and plants was significant for children in both countries who discussed the teacher directed school and the developmental psychology based school but not so important to children who were read the plan for a rights-based school. Such contact, however, is a precondition for the successful implementation of article 29(e) on an education teaching children respect for the natural environment.

The issue of a safe physical environment was not raised by children who discussed the plan for a teacher directed school in Scotland but was raised by children in Elm School and Oak School in Greece. Children who were read the plan for school based on developmental psychology, however, talked about different aspects of safety. Children in Scotland (Hill School) were concerned about fires in school, which were not included in the plan, whereas some children in Greece (Oak School and Pine School) were concerned about the protection that a hedge around the school could not provide. So, for different reasons, article 19 was important to most children in both countries. Out of the four focus groups in both countries who discussed the plan for a rights-based school, half of them did not talk about the lack of physical boundaries around the school yard (Valley School and Pine School), whereas children from Elm School and Oak School in Greece were afraid for children who would attend a school without a fence.

In general, in Scotland, only one out of the five focus groups expressed concerns about children safety in school (Hill School). In Greece, children from Oak school, regardless of the plan they discussed were afraid for their safety followed by children in two out of three focus groups in Elm School.

Children in Scotland prioritized children's right to education (article 28.1) and in particular, the education of children in relation to the development of their mental and physical abilities / capabilities (article 29(a)) and partly with children's preparation for a responsible life in a free society (article 29(d)). Children in Greece, however, emphasized article 31 on their right to play, when discussing the physical environment of a school for young children. The views of the children from both countries indicated that children had accepted the purposes of the educational provision they were offered in their countries and based their suggestions for improvement of the plan on their experience.

Children in Scotland who were read the plan for a school based on developmental psychology made some suggestions for improvement that were not mentioned by other groups in either country. Some children from the group from Hill School would add school uniforms to the school plan, whereas their peers in the same group thought that children should have the freedom to choose what to wear. These children expressed concerns about two different rights. Those who wanted school uniforms were concerned with article 2 and children's rights not to be discriminated based on what they wear. Those who wanted children to wear whatever clothes they chose were interested both in article 2 and in article 13 and children's right to freedom of expression.

The Social Environment Of a School and Children's Rights

When it comes to the social environment of the perfect school for young children, the groups from Scotland who were read the plan for a teacher-directed school were more likely to want children to be consulted about rule setting or other decisions made at school than the groups in Greece. To these children, article 12 was important but they also needed article 5 to be fully or better implemented so that children can exercise their rights. Their views indicated that the high score in indulgence may have influenced the views of children in Scotland as well as the low score in power distance. Children did not want to be restrained without their consent and consultation and they did not seem to accept their less powerful position.

In Greece, only children in Elm School who were read the plan for an authoritarian school, agreed with the idea of a teacher setting the rules on their own. The rest of them wanted to be consulted and to have a say, which means that article 12 was important to them in terms of rule-making. Furthermore, children's safety (article 19) was linked to the teachers' role in school only by children in Greece. Children in Elm School suggested that keeping children safe was the work of the teacher who makes rules for the safety of the children in their class. Children in Oak School did not want a teacher who may hit children, even though the word punishment (not beating or hitting) was used in the plan for an authoritarian school. Their views about the role of a teacher echoed not only article 19, but also article 28.2., which emphasizes the administration of discipline in a way that respects children dignity.

Out of all the children who were read the plan for a school based on developmental psychology, only two commented on rule making. Children in focus groups from Valley School in Scotland and from Oak School in Greece were in favor of children making some rules with their teachers, as the plan described.

There were four focus groups who were read the plan for a rights-based school. Children from Valley School, Scotland and from Elm School, Greece were in favor of children co-deciding the rules with their teachers. However, in Greece, the views of children in Oak School and in Pine School were split between rules being set by the teacher and rules being co-decided by children and teachers. This means that children in Greece may have been influenced by the high score of power distance as well as of collectivism in their country as compared to UK.

Half of the focus groups who were read the plan for a rights-based school agreed on children setting the rules together with their teachers (Valley School, Scotland and Elm School, Greece). The views of children from Oak School and Pine School in Greece, were split between rules being set only by the teacher and rules being set by the teacher with the children. The low score on individualism according to Hofstede (2021b) may explain why some children did not consider participation in rule setting as a matter for them to co-decide with their teachers.

Regarding who should make decisions in school, only three focus groups discussed it; two in Scotland and one in Greece. Both focus groups in Scotland (Valley School and Hill School) said they would like children as well as themselves to decide things with their teachers. On the contrary, children from Oak School in Greece believed that the teacher should make decisions at school. Therefore, children in Scotland prioritized article 12 but children in Oak School did not consider themselves capable of sharing decision-making. This indicates that a lot more action needs to be taken for the implementation of article 5 in Greece.

Main Findings of the Second Focus Group Sessions

The Perfect School for Wilson

Children in both countries wanted a lot of play resources and equipment for the perfect school for Wilson. The need for more time for play was more urgent in Scotland whereas in Greece children wanted more space for play. These differences indicate that certain features of the educational provision in each country are not in accord with children's views and needs. In Scotland, children did not believe they had enough time to play while at school so they did not want Wilson to experience such a shortage. In Greece, the low budget for education leads to poorer facilities for children and children in the groups did not wish Wilson a similar fate.

When it comes to learning in the perfect school for Wilson, half of the children in Scotland were not in favor of lessons and even suggested extra help for him in the form of a robot or a servant. Children in Greece either wanted learning or did not make any comments about it.

When comparing what children thought about play and learning, it is evident that children in Scotland wanted a more child-friendly and play-based school for Wilson than what they were offered. Children in Greece in that sense were more satisfied with the provision made for them in terms of time allocation between play and learning.

Sweets, chocolate and other sugary foods were popular in both countries but more so in Scotland. It seems that article 24 about children's right to healthy nutrition was not a priority for most of the children who discussed food at the perfect school for Wilson.

Children in both countries wanted a school for Wilson with either lax rules or with teachers who do not shout at children when they break the rules. Children in Scotland were clear about the fact that the rules in their school were overwhelming for them and did not wish the same for Wilson whereas in Greece children did not; they just blamed their teachers for overreacting (*e.g.* telling them off) when they break the rules. Some children in Scotland did not even want a teacher in the new school for Wilson. Differences in the score of indulgence could not explain the finding that children in both countries complained about school rules. Perhaps it is the power distance between children and adults and the improper implementation of articles 12, 3 and 5 in both countries that can account for children not desiring strict rules for Wilson. Children wanted to be taken seriously but to achieve that, adults should not always suppose that they know what is best for children and help children learn what they are entitled to and how to claim it.

Findings and the Convention on the Rights of the Child

What the data from both sessions in Scotland and Greece indicates is that articles 12, 19, 28, 29, and 31 were important to children in both countries but article 24 was not. They wanted to be consulted when decisions affecting them are made, they wanted to be safe from physical harm, to be educated and to play, but not to eat healthy food. Children not knowing how to claim their place in the decision-making process in school suggests that adults need to find ways to better implement article 5 and article 12 at school.

Article 2 about children right not to be discriminated was on the minds of children in both countries, but mainly of children from Greece, when they discussed a school for Wilson with other little wolves as a better option than his being in the same school with people. The right to non-discrimination was also on their minds when children from Hill School discussed children's attire at school. In this case, what became evident is that it is not always easy for the children to combine article 2 with article 13, that is, children's right not to be discriminated but to also have freedom of expression.

The findings of this study reinforce the findings of the research by Einarsdottir (2005) on what children in Iceland wanted but were not allowed to decide. Children in her study said they could not decide:

'When we go outdoors

What we have for lunch

When to leave choice time

When to leave rest time

To ruin things if the playschool teacher leaves

To run in the hallway

To sleep

To hurt other people

To change the rules

To be rude' (Einarsdottir, 2005, p. 482).

The same perceptions were recorded by this research. Children both in Greece and Scotland spoke of outdoor play a lot more than they did of playing indoors and wanted Wilson to be able to go outside whenever he wanted or the teacher to let him go to the yard more frequently than they themselves were allowed ('when we go outdoors' and 'when to leave choice time' and 'rest time' in Einarsdottir's study). They wanted the chance to decide what to eat ('what we have for lunch' in Einarsdottir's study) and to rest ('to sleep' in Einarsdottir's study) either as improvement of the plans they were read or as a feature of the perfect school for Wilson. What children, mainly in Scotland, called crazy and silly rules for a perfect school for children and for Wilson had also been recorded by Einarsdottir ('to ruin things if the playschool teacher leaves', 'to run in the hallway', 'to hurt other people', 'to change the rules', 'to be rude' in Einarsdottir's study).

The data of this study also reinforce the findings of the research by Sheridan and Pramling-Samuelsson (2001). Young children in Sweden claimed that their teachers decided almost everything, such as the conditions in schools, everyday routines, rules, norms and values, and handling little daily incidents, whereas they could not even decide where and when to play. Most of the children in this study wanted either young children and /or Wilson to have a say in the decisions made at school that affect them, such as the setting of the rules (rules, norms and values in Sheridan and Pramling-Samuelsson's study) or the choice of activities and their frequency (everyday routine for play and learning in Sheridan and Pramling-Samuelsson's study).

This means that a large part of the two pieces of research that inspired me was confirmed by this study, despite the fact that this research was conducted in Scotland and Greece and not Iceland and Sweden. Therefore, it appears that article 12 of the Convention and children's right to be consulted and participate in decision making affecting their lives, according to their ability to form opinions, is problematic in Scotland and Greece, as it was in Sweden and Iceland about twenty years ago. The same applies to article 31 and children's right to play at school and article 5 and children's right to direction and help with learning and claiming their rights. In order for children to exercise the agency foreseen for them by the Convention in its article 12, adults need to work on the implementation of articles 5 and 31 fervently.

Findings and the Conceptualizations of Schooling

Children's views in both countries showed an eclectic preference for resources and practices, which they wanted to be available to young children at school. They emphasized some aspects of all three different models of school (analyzed in Chapter 2) read to them either when they discussed each individual plan of a school or when describing their plan for a school for Wilson.

From the authoritarian model of schooling, some of the children in both countries kept the need for tidiness and cleanness (Ciccelli, 1983; MacNaughton, 2020), worksheets and learning the basics (Lowe, 2007) as well as the need for an adult to tell them what to do and how to behave (Ross, 2008, p. 115, as cited in Brown, 2014, p. 7), even though the last element was raised more in Greece. Most of the children in both countries would not keep the teacher of this model who decides about everything on her own and punishes children (Archard, 2004). This was also evident in their descriptions of the role of a teacher for the perfect school for Wilson.

From the model of schooling based on developmental psychology, children in both countries considered setting some of the school rules with their teachers and deciding with her about some other matters affecting them at school (Bruce, 1997; Singer, 1996; Warner & Lynch, 2004) as important, even though these matters were not clear in their mind. They would also keep its resources (Curtis, 1998), but not necessarily their hedge around the yard due to their fears of physical harm (Jans, 2004), particularly in Greece. They did not consider a teacher playing with them as necessary and that was true for the rights-based school, too, and their descriptions of the perfect school for Wilson.

What some children could not accept about a rights-based school was that there were no physical boundaries to the schoolyard due to the fear of their safety (mainly in Greece) and the idea that play would not be interrupted by teachers for lessons (in Scotland). Furthermore, not all children in both countries agreed with the idea of children co-deciding about all school matters with their teachers at school (Aldreson, 2008; Howe & Covell, 2005; Osler & Starkey, 1998), which was not even touched upon in the sessions about Wilson's school. Despite the fact that the plan for a rights-based school had more resources than the other two models, children in both countries (more so in Greece) had more suggestions for play and learning equipment, which was clearer when discussing the perfect school for Wilson.

It is evident that children in both countries, despite the different types of education provided to them, had already acquired some features of being a pupil. In the best school ever, lessons were to be offered and even suggestions for changing the topics, the materials or the pedagogy were given. All school matters and all behavior issues were not considered part of their role as children or pupils in a school in their respective countries. Teachers were there to protect them from their *destructive* nature (Walkerdine & Lucey, 1989, as cited in Burman, 2008, p. 269) and teach them to be socially adjusted to the ethos of schools in their countries (Burman, 2008; Lowe, 2007).

All kinds of resources for child-initiated activities were deemed essential for a perfect school for young children, without distinguishing them as play or learning materials. What I recorded in both countries is children requesting materials some of which were clearly related to play. For example, they used the term *toys*. However, they refered to other objects or facilities, which can be used either for playful, teacher-organized activities (*e.g.* reading books or using the computers to acquaint children with a new story) as well as objects and facilities that can be either used by teachers or by children and therefore, they cannot be unquestionably named play / child directed activities resources or teaching materials (*e.g.* books and tablets). This could be due to children having accepted their role as pupils, in either primary school or kindergarten, who need to learn.

It could also be due to the possibility that children were not really functioning within the dichotomy between play and work / lesson / learning (Howard, 2010). Breathnach, Danby and O'Gorman (2017) have also recorded activities that children undertook, which were neither teacher-directed (lessons) nor 'ordinarily categorized as play' (Breathnach, Danby and O'Gorman, 2017, p. 446). They employ the term 'inside play' to show a period of time, when a child 'can choose an activity; in other words, a time and context where she could assert agency' (Breathnach, Danby, & O'Gorman, 2017, p. 447). Writing as a freely chosen activity was one of the examples they observed. Children found writing assigned to them by the teacher boring but they were interested in engaging in writing when their self initiated activities demanded it; for example, writing a label for their shop. In their study, children did not categorize activities as play or work based on the criterion of an adult's presence or absence, when the activities were carried out, as other researchers have (Keating, Fabian, Jordan, Mavers, & Roberts, 2000). The findings draw our attention to taking into account the children's own agenda and 'planning *with* children' (Breathnach, Danby, & O'Gorman, 2017, p. 450; see also Katz, 1986).

What become apparent from the children's views is that some of them still needed to play at the age of 5 years without necessarily rejecting learning what their teachers taught them. For some children there was no balance between learning and play (Hurst, 1991; Wood and Attfiled, 1996), whereas others, especially in Scotland, felt comfortable with the daily routine of their school. This is in accordance with other research on children transitioning to primary school who consider it a place of work and not of play any more (Corsaro & Molinari, 2000; Fisher 2009). In both countries, the children's suggestions for material resources indicates, apart for the need for more play, the need for more hands-on, palpable activities and choices for children aged 5 years (Bruce, 1997; Curtis, 1998) and, therefore, the need for a change in the pedagogy employed by teachers of young children.

These two findings are in accordance both with the conceptualization of a school based on developmental psychology as well as a rights based school. Both types of schools for young children claim to cater for the need for a child centered education especially in early childhood. However, only the rights based schools allow children to have the control they need or want to exert on matters such as their play and their learning. This control is not defined by the developmental stage children are found in, according to traditional developmental psychology, but by the acknowledgement of children as rights holders (Lundy & McEvoy, 2012).

Children's Rights, School and Play

Children's suggestions for resources for their self-initiated activities led me to examine General Comment No. 17 on the right of the child to rest, leisure, play, recreational activities, cultural life and the arts (art. 31)* (2013, GC 17 henceforth). This document cites perspectives on children's play coming from Developmental Psychology and Early Childhood Education, which are two of the main scientific fields studying child's play and advocating play especially for the youngest children (*e.g.* GC 17, 2013, pp. 4-5 & 10-11). It refers to the contribution of play to 'creativity, physical, emotional, social and intellectual development, imagination and self-confidence' (GC 17, 2013, p. 4).

GC 17 suggests areas of improvement that every Member State must consider in order to facilitate the implementation of children's right to play, leisure and cultural life. Public awareness of the significance of play is requested by the Comment as well as the participation of children in the design of play related facilities (GC 17, 2013, pp. 17-20). When it comes to schools, it suggests their daily schedule allows time for arts and games and the establishment of safe yet free enough from the adult gaze playgrounds for children to play in. Homework should not be overwhelming and pedagogy should be more playful (GC 17, 2013, pp. 21-22).

However, it does not reach the core of the significance of play to human development nor the deeper reasons play is undervalued or underrepresented in schools nowadays. Such a conceptualization of play would clarify misunderstandings about its value and facilitate play-related changes.

Peter Gray, an evolutionary developmental psychologist who has also studied works from anthropology and history, gives an impressive example of the meaning and significance of free play for children in general, and not only for the younger ones, in his book *Free to Learn* (2013). Gray's definition of free play is 'play in which the players themselves decide what and how to play and are free to modify the goals and rules as they go along' (Gray, 2013, p. 7). Such play is considered a natural predisposition, which helps children feel 'that they are not helpless' (Gray, 2013, p. 17). Free play teaches children 'to learn to make their own decisions, solve their own problems, create and abide by rules and get along with others' (Gray, 2013, p. 17); lessons from play already discussed in academia (*e.g.*Bordova & Leong, 2011; Grieshaber & McArdle, 2010; Smith, 2010; Wood, 2010). However, what Gray adds to these outcomes of free play is that children learn to get along with others 'as equals rather than as obedient or rebellious subordinates' (Gray, 2013, pp. 17-18). When free play is social, that is played with others, benefits added to the catalog of play advantages are that children learn to pay attention to the needs of others (as well as their own) and make decisions consensually (Gray, 2013, p. 34). Such free play, especially when it is social, is the natural way in which children become competent in claiming their right to participation as defined in article 12 of the Convention, because, in free social play, children learn to form opinions (necessary for the enjoyment of article 12), express them (in accordance with article 13) and participate in decision making that is meaningful to them (*i.e.* matters affecting their lives of article 12).

Furthermore, some of the children's idea about a school for wolves only as the best solution for Wilson or for the same school attire for all children in the best school ever indicated that children were concerned about discrimination based on diversity, in terms of species segregation and bullying over dressing. However, one of the features of free social play is that by its nature is all-inclusive. 'It helps children learn how to treat one another RESPECTFULLY, AS EQUALS in ways that meet EVERYONE'S needs and desires, DESPITE DIFFERENCES IN SIZE, STRENGTH AND ABILITY[1] ' (Gray, 2013, p. 34). This means that free social play can contribute to the implementation of article 2 and children's right to non discrimination.

Gray also offers a different perspective on how schools operate, which he relates to the reasons free play has left schools, even schools for the youngest children. He analyzes at least seven features of the existing education systems in the West world (part of which are Greece and Scotland), which deny children their freedom and its main manifestation; free play. Schools (1) deny children their liberty without just cause, (2) interfere with the development of each child's sense of responsibility, the development of their self-direction, (3) interfere with children's cooperation with each other, (4) turn learning into a boring job, thus killing children's intrinsic motivation, (5) judge children's bad performance in a shameproducing manner, (6) hinder the development of critical thinking in children and (7) reduce the diversity of knowledge and skills children develop.

In this study, children wanted more play and their descriptions indicated some of the aspects of schooling Gray considers as real and as existing together with the squeezing of play out of the daily routine of schools in the West^2 . The children in both countries who participated in this research were willing to learn what the teacher has chosen for them and in the ways the teacher chose, but to a certain extent. Despite the fact that children at age 5 years were in kindergartens in Greece, they, too, as well as children in Scotland, who were in primary schools, wanted more play either in terms of time or of materials. They wanted more materials for play and focused mainly on play and their self-selected activities either alone or with others, which indicates that they needed to cultivate their self-direction, self-regulation and autonomy. Asking for more play or play resources was also a way for them to say that they still had motivation to learn but in the way nature has endowed them. That is even more so for the few children in Scotland who would add real life materials to their lessons in language and maths (*e.g.* texts from periodicals as reading material).

It is as if they were saying that school denied them their freedom because they could play only during breaks, even though in Greece there was time for freely chosen activities in the daily routine of the kindergarten. School denied them their freedom, because the children in this study wanted to participate in decision making but they were not asked to do so or they did not know how to claim this right. Their critique of teachers' shouting at them and their suggestions for acceptable behaviors on their teachers' part and for classroom rules were their way of saying that they did not want to be ridiculed, instead of helped to learn learn how to operate and co-operate with others.

Throughout the analysis of the data I have maintained that the implementation of article 5 was crucial in accomplishing children acting as rights holders. However, when it comes to young children, like the 5 to 6 year olds participating in this study, one finds that for children to learn that they are right holders and how to be right holders, we need to let them develop and learn through their free play rather than first criple their freedom (in schools and other environments with no free play or limited play) and then attempt to fix them (the children)! And it appears that this is a problem whether the school young children attend is a primary school or a kindergarten. It is amazing how children in Greece, whose education did not include teaching them to read and write and whose half of their daily time in kindergarten was to be dedicated to free activities, have complained about the violation of their right to play as much as children in Scotland who were in a primary class and obliged to learn the 3R's! Despite the different education provisions for the participants and the fact that one would expect children in Greece to be happier with their more time to play and their less academic curriculum, there was something in both institutions (primary and preschool) that did not satisfy children's need for free play and for choices. Therefore, the provision in both countries did not provide adequately for play as a developmental and natural need and did not provide children with opportunities to self-direct their learning and to act as rights holders. They were deprived of the leading activity, as Vygotsky (1966) called play, which gives them the opportunity to realize what they know and what they need to know, to learn how to negotiate with others so that they naturally aquire ways of thinking, acting, and participating. That is, children were deprived of the natural way right holders learn and claim their participation rights, FREE PLAY!

Implications of the Study

The findings of this research are useful to teachers as well as policymakers. Teachers can begin to consider if their practices are similar to the ones children favored or not and attempt to improve them. They need to consider if they can allow more scope for consultation and children's participation in decision-making, especially when it comes to setting the rules or defining them. Another issue they need to consider is the daily routine and allowing children more time for play and other child-initiated activities.

Policymakers can withhold or modify the strictness and rigidness of existing policies, which interfere with the implementation of children's rights, other than that of education, at schools. Further professional development for teachers as well as policymakers emerges as a significant factor for the creation of a school promoting respect to, protection of and fulfillment of children's rights.

The issue of a (un)healthy diet, which was brought up by the children, is another matter that needs to be examined, so that measures can be taken to protect children health more effectively.

Further Research on the Topic

This is an exploratory research on young children's views on education for children of their age in Scotland and Greece. The views of more children can be produced in both countries as well as in other countries especially if their education system is distinctly different from the Scottish and the Greek, *e.g.* of Denmark, Finland or Japan and China.

The methodology of the research could also be varied. Instead of using only an oral method of producing data (*i.e.* focus groups), a method like that of Gripton and Vincent (2020) can be useful. They gave children small-world toys to gain insight into their experiences of school. Perhaps the perfect school for Wilson or for 5 year olds can be discussed and depicted by children. Gundarina (2020) also used props, such as board games, to facilitate her interviews with children. Whether further research will use focus groups or interviews, props should be employed to facilitate the expression of children's views.

It would also be interesting to see how teachers feel about children's views on education and how well-prepared they think they are to facilitate the implementation of children's rights at school.

All the above emphasize the importance of conducting comparative research in education. Despite the differences in budgets, educational provision and dimensions of their national cultures, the comparative nature of this study indicated two major similarities in children's views: children's desire (a) for less control by adults over them and (b) for more play and initiative for children in school. Comparative Education is alive and a worthwhile endeavor!

NOTES

[1] The capitalization of keywords is my emphasis.

[2] Similar understanding of free play in non-western countries have been recorded by other play experts. An example can be found in Marfo and Biersteker's chapter (2011, pp. 73-85) entitled 'Exploring culture, play, and early childhood education practice in African contexts'.

REFERENCES

Alderson, P. (2008). *Young children's rights: Exploring beliefs, principles and practice.* Jessica Kingsley.

Aman, R. (2018). *Decolonising Intercultural Education: Colonial differences, the geopolitics of knowledge and inter-epistemic dialogue.* Routledge.

Archard, D. (2004). *Children: Rights and childhood.* (5th ed) Routledge.

Archard, D., & Skivenes, M. (2009). Balancing a child's best interests and a child's views. *Int. J. Child. Rights, 17*(1), 1-21.
[http://dx.doi.org/10.1163/157181808X358276]

Arnstein, S.R. (1969). A ladder of citizen participation. *J. Am. Inst. Plann., 35*(4), 216-224.
[http://dx.doi.org/10.1080/01944366908977225]

Berrell, M. (2020). *National culture and the social relations of anywhere working.* https://www.igi-global.com/chapter/national-culture-and-the-social-relations-of-anywhere-working/263827

Blenkin, G.V., & Kelly, A.V. (1997). *Principles into practice in early childhood education.* Paul Chapman.

Burts, D.C., Charlesworth, R., Fleege, P.O., Hart, C.H., Mosley, J., & Thomasson, R.H. (1992). Observed activities and stress behaviors of children in developmentally appropriate and inappropriate kindergarten classrooms. *Early Child. Res. Q., 7*(2), 297-318.
[http://dx.doi.org/10.1016/0885-2006(92)90010-V]

Bordova, E., & Leong, D.J. (2011). Revisiting Vygotskian perspectives on play and pedagogy. In S. Rogers (Ed.), *Rethinking play and pedagogy in early childhood education: Concepts, contexts and cultures* (pp. 60-72). Routledge.

Bouzakis, S. (1993). Sigritiki Pedagogiki III / Συγκριτική Παιδαγωγική III [Comparative education III]. Gutenberg.

Bowe, R., Ball, S.J., & Gold, A. (1992). *Reforming education and changing schools: Case studies in policy sociology.* Routledge.

Breathnach, H., Danby, S., & O'Gorman, L. (2017). 'Are you working or playing?' Investigating young children's perspectives of classroom activities. *Int. J. Early Years Educ., 25*(4), 439-454.
[http://dx.doi.org/10.1080/09669760.2017.1316241]

Broadfoot, P., Osborn, M., with Gilly, M., & Bûcher, A. (1993). *Perceptions of teaching: Primary school teachers in England and France.* Cassell.

Brown, M. A. (2014). What is childhood? In: M. A. Brown & J. White (Eds.), *Exploring childhood in a comparative context: An introductory guide for students* (pp. 5-15). Routledge.

Bruce, T. (1997). *Early childhood education* (2nd ed.). Hodder and Stoughton.

Burman, E. (2008). *Deconstructing developmental psychology* (2nd ed.). Routledge.

Calogiannaki, P. (2011). *Sigritiki pedagogiki: Epistimologika ke methodologika zitimata / Συγκριτική Παιδαγωγική: Επιστημολογικά και μεθοδολογικά ζητήματα* [Comparative Education: Epistemological and methodological issues]. Ion.

Calogiannaki, P. (2015). *Peri Sigritikis Pedagogikis / Περί συγκριτικής παιδαγωγικής* [About Comparative Education]. Gutenber.

Cicchelli, T. (1983). Forms and functions of instruction patterns: Direct and nondirect. *Instr. Sci., 12*(4), 343-353.
[http://dx.doi.org/10.1007/BF00154125]

Clarkson, J. (2009). What is comparative education? In W. Bignold & L. Gayton (Eds.), *Global issues and comparative education* (pp. 4-17). Sag.

Cohen, L., Manion, L., & Morrison, K. (2018). *Research methods in education* (8th ed.). Routledge.

Collins (n.d.). Equal. In Collins Online Dictionary https://www.collins dictionary.com/dictionary/english/equal

Colucci, E. (2007). "Focus groups can be fun": The use of activity-oriented questions in focus group discussions. *Qual. Health Res., 17*(10), 1422-1433.
[http://dx.doi.org/10.1177/1049732307308129] [PMID: 18000081]

Corsaro, W.A., & Molinari, L. (2000). Priming events and Italian children's transition from preschool to elementary school: Representations and actions. *Soc. Psychol. Q., 63*(1), 16-33.
[http://dx.doi.org/10.2307/2695878]

Cornwall, A. (2008). Unpacking participation models, meanings and practices. *Community Development Journal, 43*(3), 269-283.
[http://dx.doi.org/10.1093/cdj/bsn010]

Covell, K., & Howe, R.B. (2001). Moral Education through the 3 Rs: Rights, respect and responsibility. *J. Moral Educ., 30*(1), 29-41.
[http://dx.doi.org/10.1080/03057240120033794]

Covell, K., Howe, R.B., & McNeil, J.K. (2010). Implementing children's human rights education in schools. *Improving Schools, 13*(2), 117-132.
[http://dx.doi.org/10.1177/1365480210378942]

Cunningham, H. (2005). *Children and childhood in western society since 1500*. Pearson Education Limited.

Cunningham, H. (2006). *The invention of childhood*. BBC Books.

Curtis, A. (1998). *A curriculum for the pre-school child: Learning to learn* (2nd ed). Routledge Falmer.

Darling, J. (2004). Scottish primary education: Philosophy and practice. In T. G. K. Bryce & W. H. Humes (Eds.), *Scottish education: Post evolution* (2nd ed., pp. 27-36). Edinburgh; University Press.

Devine, D. (1999). Children: Rights and status in education - A socio-historical analysis. Irish Educational Studies, 18(1), 14-28.
[http://dx.doi.org/10.1080/0332331990180105]

Einarsdottir, J. (2005). We can decide what to play! Children's perception of quality in an Icelandic playschool. *Early Educ. Dev., 16*(4), 469-488.
[http://dx.doi.org/10.1207/s15566935eed1604_7]

Eldén, S. (2013). Inviting the messy: Drawing methods and 'children's voices'. *Childhood, 20*(1), 66-81.

[http://dx.doi.org/10.1177/0907568212447243]

Farlane, A. (2018). *China, Japan, Europe and the Anglo-sphere: A comparative analysis*. Cam Rivers Publishing.

Filias, V. (1989). *Kinoniologikes prosegisis / Κοινωνιολογικές προσεγγίσεις* [Sociological approaches]. Sihroni Epoh.

Fisher, J.A. (2009). 'We used to play in Foundation, it was more funner': investigating feelings about transition from Foundation Stage to Year 1. *Early Years J. Int. Res. Dev., 29*(2), 131-145.
[http://dx.doi.org/10.1080/09575140802672576]

Flewitt, R. (2005). Conducting research with young children: Some ethical considerations. *Early Child Dev. Care, 175*(6), 553-565.
[http://dx.doi.org/10.1080/03004430500131338]

Flick, U. (2007). The sage qualitative research kit. Designing qualitative research. *Sage.*

Francis, M., & Lorenzo, R. (2002). Seven realms of children's participation. *J. Environ. Psychol., 22*(1-2), 157-169.
[http://dx.doi.org/10.1006/jevp.2001.0248]

Freeman, E.B., & Hatch, J.A. (1989). What schools expect young children to know and do: An analysis of kindergarten report cards. *Elem. Sch. J., 89*(5), 595-605.
[http://dx.doi.org/10.1086/461594]

Georgeson, J., Payler, J., & Cambell-Barr, V. (2013). The importance of international perspectives. In: J. Georgeson & J. Payler (Eds.), *International perspectives of early childhood education and care* (pp. 3-8). Open University Press.

Gibson, F. (2007). Conducting focus groups with children and young people: Strategies for success. *J. Res. Nurs., 12*(5), 473-483.
[http://dx.doi.org/10.1177/1744987107079791]

Gizeli, V. D. (1987). *Deka mathimata stin kinoniologia / Δέκα μαθήματα στην κοινωνιολογία* [Ten lessons in Sociology]. Epikerotit.

Goecke, N. (1976). What do they mean by 'Back to Basics'? *Music Educators J., 63*(3), 30-33.
[http://dx.doi.org/10.2307/3395094]

Gotowos, A. (1983). *Piotiki erevna stis epistimes tis agogis / Ποιοτική έρευνα στις επιστήμες της αγωγής* [Qualitative research in education sciences]. Dodoni.

Gray, P. (2013). *Free to learn. Why unleashing the instinct to play will make our children happier, more self-reliant, and better students for life*. Basic Books.

Green, A. (1990). Education and state formation. The rise of education systems in England, France and the USA. Palgrave.

Grieshaber, S., & McArdle, F. (2010). *The trouble with play*. McGraw Hill.

Gripton, C., & Vincent, K. (2020). Using small world toys for research: a method for gaining insight into children's lived experiences of school. *Int. J. Res. Method Educ., 44*(3), 225-240.
[http://dx.doi.org/10.1080/1743727X.2020.1753692]

Gundarina, O. (2020). Interviews with creative techniques: research with Russian-speaking migrant pupils. *Int. J. Res. Method Educ.,* *44*(4), 414-432.
[http://dx.doi.org/10.1080/1743727X.2020.1804543]

Hall, E.L., & Kofkin Rudkin, J. (2011). *Seen and heard: Children's rights in early childhood education.* Teachers College Press.

Hart, C. (2014). *Whiffy Wilson: The wolf who wouldn't go to school.* Orchard Books.

Hartley, D. (1993). *Understanding the nursery school.* Cassell.

Hatch, A. J. (1995). (Ed). *Qualitative research in early childhood settings.* Praeger Publisher.

Hedegaard, M. (2008). A cultural-historical theory of children's development. In M. Hedegaard & M. Fleer (Eds.), *Studying children: A cultural-historical approach* (pp. 10-29). OU.

Hellenic Republic (2021). Kratikos proipologismos / Κρατικός προϋπολογισμός [State Budget]. (2021). https://www.minfin.gr/documents/20182/14940417/%CE%9A%CE%A1%CE%91%CE%A4%CE%99%CE%9A%CE%9F%CE%A3+%CE%A0%CE%A1%CE%9F%CE%A5%CE%A0%CE%9F%CE%9B%CE%9F%CE%93%CE%99%CE%A3%CE%9C%CE%9F%CE%A3+2021.pdf/90427c6f-d2a2-421e-9-87-6e5d5685b9fe.

Hofstede, G. (2019a, February 3). *National culture.* https://www.hofstede-insights.com/models/national-culture/

Hofstede, G. (2019b, February 3). *Compare countries.* https://www.hofstede-insights.com/product/compare-countries/

Hofstede, G. (2021a, January 5). *National culture.* https://hi.hofstede-insights.com/national-culture

Hofstede, G. (2021b, January 5). *Country comparison.* https://www.hofstede-insights.com/country-comparison/greece,the-uk/

Howard, J. (2010). Making the most of play in the early years: The importance of children's perceptions. In: P. Broadhead J. Howard & E. Wood (Eds.), *Play and learning in the early years* (pp. 145-160). Sage.

Howe, R.B., & Covell, K. (2005). Miseducating children about their rights. *Educ. Citizsh. Soc. Justice,* *5*(2), 91-102.
[http://dx.doi.org/10.1177/1746197910370724]

Hughes, P. (2001). Paradigms, methods and knowledge. In: G. MacNaughton S. A. Rolfe & I. Siraj-Blatchford (Eds.), *Doing early childhood research: International perspectives on theory and practice* (pp. 31-55). Allen and Unwi.

Hurst, V. (1991). *Planning for early learning: Education in the first five years.* Paul Chapman.

International Save the Children Alliance. (2007). *Getting it right for children: A practitioners' guide to child rights programming.* Save the Children UK.

James, A. (2007). Giving voice to children's voices: Practices and problems, pitfalls and potentials. *Am. Anthropol.,* *109*(2), 261-272.
[http://dx.doi.org/10.1525/aa.2007.109.2.261]

Jans, M. (2004). Children as citizens: Towards a contemporary notion of child participation. *Childhood,*

11(1), 27-44.
[http://dx.doi.org/10.1177/0907568204040182]

Johnny, L. (2005). UN Convention on the rights of the child: A rationale for implementing participatory rights in schools. *Can. J. Educ. Adm. Policy, 40*(May), 1-20. http://iej.cjb.net

Johnson, L., & van Wyk, M. (2016). Approaches to teaching EMS: The teacher-centred approach. In: M. van Wyk & K. dos Reis (Eds.), *Teaching Economics and Management Sciences in the Senior Phase* (pp. 103-120). Oxford University Press.

Jones, P. (2011a). What are children's rights? Contemporary developments and debates. In: P. Jones & G. Walker (Eds.), *Children's rights in practice* (pp. 2-16). Sage.
[http://dx.doi.org/10.4135/9781473914711.n1]

Jones, P. (2011b). Participation and provision across disciplines: Child rights for, and by, children. In: P. Jones & G. Walker (Eds.), *Children's rights in practice* (pp. 43-56). Sage.
[http://dx.doi.org/10.4135/9781473914711.n4]

Jones, P., & Welsh, S. (2018). *Rethinking children's rights: Attitudes in contemporary society.* (2nd ed). Bloomsbury.
[http://dx.doi.org/10.5040/9781350001282]

Kaime, T. (2011). *The convention on the rights of the child: A cultural legitimacy critique.* Europa Law Publishing.

Kalantzis, M., Cope, B., & Harvey, A. (2003). Assessing multiliteracies and the new basics. *Asess. Educ., 10*(1), 15-26.
[http://dx.doi.org/10.1080/09695940301692]

Kanyal, M. (2014). Childhood and children's participation: A social – cultural perspective. In: M. Kanyal (Ed.), *Children's rights 0-8: Promoting participation in education and care* (pp. 26-41). Routledge.
[http://dx.doi.org/10.4324/9781315815107]

Kanyal, M., & Gibbs, J. (2014). Participation: Why and how? In: M. Kanyal (Ed.), *Children's rights 0-8: Promoting participation in education and care* (pp. 45-62). Routledge.
[http://dx.doi.org/10.4324/9781315815107]

Katz, C. (1986). Children and the environment: Work, play and learning in rural Sudan. *Child. Environ. Q., 3*(4), 43-51.

Kay-Flowers, S. (2009). Education and social care: friends or foes? In: W. Bignold & l. Gayton (Eds.), *Global Issues and Comparative Education* (pp. 94-108). Sage..

Kazamias, A. M. (2009). Forgotten men, forgotten themes: The historical-philosophical-cultural and liberal humanist motif in Comparative Education. In: R. Cowen & A. M. Kazamias (Eds.), *International Handbook of Comparative Education* (pp. 37-58). Springer.
[http://dx.doi.org/10.1007/978-1-4020-6403-6_4]

Keating, I., Fabian, H., Jordan, P., Mavers, D., & Roberts, J. (2000). "Well, I've not done any work today. I don't know why I came to school". Perceptions of play in reception class. *Educ. Stud., 26*(4), 437-454.
[http://dx.doi.org/10.1080/03055690020003638]

Keesing, R.M. (1974). Theories of Culture. *Annu. Rev. Anthropol., 3*, 73-97.
[http://dx.doi.org/10.1146/annurev.an.03.100174.000445]119

Kitzinger, J. (1994). The methodology of Focus Groups: the importance of interaction between research participants. *Sociol. Health Illn., 16*(1), 103-121.
[http://dx.doi.org/10.1111/1467-9566.ep11347023]

Kitzinger, J. (1995). Qualitative Research: Introducing focus groups. *BMJ, 311*(7000), 299-302.
[http://dx.doi.org/10.1136/bmj.311.7000.299] [PMID: 7633241]

Kok-Aun, T. (2014). Teacher-centred teaching is alive and well. *Teaching and Learning, 15*(1), 12-17.
http://hdl.handle.net/10497/440

Lancy, D.F. (2012). Unmasking children's agency. *AnthropoChildren*, 2(October), 1-20. Corpus ID: 170186959.

Large, A., & Beheshti, J. (2001). Focus groups with children: Do they work? *Can. J. Inf. Lib. Sci., 26*(2), 86-89.

Lee, N. (1998). Towards an immature sociology. *Sociol. Rev., 46*(3), 458-482.
[http://dx.doi.org/10.1111/1467-954X.00127]

Leininger, E.V. (1979). Back to basics: Underlying concepts and controversy. *Elem. Sch. J., 79*(3), 167-173.
[http://dx.doi.org/10.1086/461147]

Leithwood, K. (1992). The move toward transformational leadership. *Educ. Leadersh., 49*(5), 8-12.

Leithwood, K., Harris, A., & Hopkins, D. (2008). Seven strong claims about successful school leadership. *Sch. Leadersh. Manage., 28*(1), 27-42.
[http://dx.doi.org/10.1080/13632430701800060]

Li, L. (2022). Developing a pedagogy of play: toddlers' conceptual learning in a PlayWorld. *Early Years J. Int. Res. Dev., 42*(3), 278-292.
[http://dx.doi.org/10.1080/09575146.2020.1739002]

Lincoln, Y.S., & Guba, E.G. *Lincoln and Guba's evaluative criteria.* http://www.qualres. org/HomeLinc-3684.html. (1985).

Lowe, R. (2007). *The death of progressive education, how teachers lost control of the classroom.* Routledge.
[http://dx.doi.org/10.4324/9780203945957]

Lubeck, S. (1995). Policy issues in the development of child care and early education systems: The need for cross national comparison. In A. J. Hatch (Ed.), *Qualitative Research in Early Childhood Settings* (pp. 79-98). Praeger.

Lundy, L. (2007). 'Voice' is not enough: Conceptualizing article 12 of the United Nations convention on the rights of the child. *Br. Educ. Res. J., 33*(6), 927-942.
[http://dx.doi.org/10.1080/01411920701657033]

Lundy, L., & McEvoy, L. (2012). Children's rights and research processes: Assisting children to (in)formed views. *Childhood, 19*(1), 129-144.
[http://dx.doi.org/10.1177/0907568211409078]

Lynch, K. (2014). New Managerialism: The Impact on education. *Concept, 5*(3), 1-11.
[http://dx.doi.org/10.13140/RG.2.1.4342.3128]

MacNaughton, G. (2020). *Shaping early childhood: Perceptions about learning, curriculum and the education context* [Shaping early childhood: Learners, curriculum and contexts]. (Y. Scarveli, Trans.). Pedio. (Original work published 2003).

MacNaughton, G., Hughes, P., & Smith, K. (2007). Young children's rights and public policy: Practices and possibilities for citizenship in the Early Years. *Child. Soc., 21*(6), 458-469.
[http://dx.doi.org/10.1111/j.1099-0860.2007.00096.x]

Mandell, N. (1991). The least-adult role in studying children. In: F.C., Waksler, (Ed.), *Studying the Social Worlds of Children: Sociological Readings* (pp. 38-59). Falmer.

Marfo, K., & Biersteker, L. (2011). Exploring culture, play, and early childhood education practice in African contexts. In: S. Rogers (Ed.), *Rethinking play and pedagogy in early childhood education: Concepts, contexts and cultures* (pp. 73-85). Routledg.

Mascolo, M.E. (2009). Beyond student - centered and teacher - centered pedagogy: Teaching and learning as guided participation. *Pedagogy and the Human Sciences, 1*(1), 3-27.

Merriam, S.B. (1995). What can you tell from an N of 1? Issues of validity and reliability in qualitative research. *PAACE J. Lifelong Learn., 4*, 51-60.

Morgan, M.T., & Robinson, N. (1976). The 'back to basics' movement in education. *Can. J. Educ., 1*(2), 1-11.
[http://dx.doi.org/10.2307/1494485]

Noble, H., & Smith, J. (2015). Issues of validity and reliability in qualitative research. *Evid. Based Nurs., 18*(2), 34-35.
[http://dx.doi.org/10.1136/eb-2015-102054] [PMID: 25653237]

Osler, A., & Starkey, H. (1998). Children's rights and citizenship: Some implications for the management of schools. *Int. J. Child. Rights, 6*(3), 313-333.
[http://dx.doi.org/10.1163/15718189820494085]

Percy-Smith, B. (2009). Beyond the UNCRC: Realising children's participation in practice. In: Children's Rights Conference: Easier said than done: 20 years of children's rights between law and practice, 11-12th June 2009, Institute of Child Health, University College London. (unpublished).

Percy-Smith, B. (2010). Councils, consultations and community: Rethinking the spaces for children and young people's participation1. *Child. Geogr., 8*(2), 107-122.
[http://dx.doi.org/10.1080/14733281003691368]

Phillips, D., & Schweisfurth, M. (2011). Comparative and International Education: An introduction to theory, method, and practice. *Continuum.*

Popkewitz, T. S., & Bloch, M. N. (2001). Administering freedom: A history of the present - Rescuing the parent to rescue the child for society. In K. Hultqvist & G. Dahlberg (Eds.), *Governing the child in the new millennium* (pp. 85-118). Routledge.

Potts, P. (2007). The place of experience in comparative education research. In: M. Bray B. Adamson & M. Mason (Eds.), *Comparative Education research: Approaches and methods* (pp. 63-81). Springer.
[http://dx.doi.org/10.1007/978-1-4020-6189-9_3]

Pugh, G. (1996). *Contemporary issues in the early years: Working collaboratively for children.* (2nd ed). Paul Chapman.

Quennerstedt, A., Quennerstedt, M. (2014). Researching children's rights in education: Sociology of

childhood encountering educational theory. *Br. J. Sociol. Educ., 35*(1), 115-132.
[http://dx.doi.org/10.1080/01425692.2013.783962]

Robinson, N. (1999). The use of focus group methodology — with selected examples from sexual health research. *J. Adv. Nurs., 29*(4), 905-913.
[http://dx.doi.org/10.1046/j.1365-2648.1999.00966.x] [PMID: 10215982]

Robson, C. (2007). *How to do a research project: A guide for undergraduate students.* Blackwell.

Ross, E.V. (1980). Back to basics: Underlying concepts and controversy. *Elem. Sch. J., 79*(3), 167-173.

Samovar, L.A., Porter, R.E., McDaniel, E.R., & Roy, C.S. (2013). *Communication between cultures.* (8th ed.). Wadsworth Cengate Learning.

Sandelowski, M. (1993). Rigor or rigor mortis: The problem of rigor in qualitative research revisited. *Advances in Nursing Science*, 16(2), 1-8.
[http://dx.doi.org/10.1097/00012272-199312000-00002] [PMID: 8311428]

Scott, W.R. (2008). Lords of the dance: Professionals as institutional agents. *Organ. Stud., 29*(2), 219-238.
[http://dx.doi.org/10.1177/0170840607088151]

Scottish Government. (2021). *Scottish Budget 2021 to 2022.* https://www.gov.scot/publications/scottish-budget-2021-22/pages/9/

Sevón, E. (2015). Who's got the power? Young children's power and agency in the child-parent relationship. *International Journal of Child, Youth and Family Studies, 6*(4.1), 622-645.
[http://dx.doi.org/10.18357/ijcyfs.641201515049]

Shenton, A.K. (2004). Strategies for ensuring trustworthiness in qualitative research projects. *Educ. Inf., 22*(2), 63-75.
[http://dx.doi.org/10.3233/EFI-2004-22201]

Sheridan, S., & Pramling-Samuelsson, I. (2001). Children's conceptions of participation and influence in preschool: A perspective on pedagogical quality. *Contemp. Issues Early Child., 2*(2), 169-194.
[http://dx.doi.org/10.2304/ciec.2001.2.2.4]

Singer, E. (1996). Prisoners of the method breaking open the child-centred pedagogy in day care centres. *Int. J. Early Years Educ., 4*(2), 28-40.
[http://dx.doi.org/10.1080/0966976960040203]

Sirkko, R., Kyrönlampi, T., & Puroila, A.M. (2019). Children's agency: Opportunities and constraints. *Int. J. Early Child., 51*(3), 283-300.
[http://dx.doi.org/10.1007/s13158-019-00252-5]

Smith, A., Duncan, J., & Marshall, K. (2005). Children's perspectives on their learning: Exploring methods. *Early Child Dev. Care, 175*(6), 473-487.
[http://dx.doi.org/10.1080/03004430500131270]

Smith, P.K. (2010). *Children and Play.* Wiley-Blackwell.

Smylie, M.A., & Eckert, J. (2018). Beyond superheroes and advocacy: The pathway of teacher leadership development. *Educ. Manage. Adm. Leadersh., 46*(4), 556-577.
[http://dx.doi.org/10.1177/1741143217694893]

Socolova, M. A., Kouzmina, E. H., & Rodionof, M. L. (1990). Comparative Education [СРАВНИТЕЛЬНАЯ

ПЕДАГОГИКА]. (A. Koutsoukalis, C. Kenourgios, & Y. Labrakis, Trans.). Sihroni Epohi. (Original work published 1978).

Stoecklin, D. (2013). Theories of action in the field of child participation: In search of explicit frameworks. *Childhood, 20*(4), 443-457.
[http://dx.doi.org/10.1177/0907568212466901]

Stolp, S. (1994). Leadership for school culture. *ERIC Digest*, 91, 1-7. Accessed January 31, 2020. https://files.eric.ed.gov/fulltext/ED370198.pdf.

Straus, A.L., & Corbin, J.M. (1998). Basics of Qualitative Research: Techniques and procedures for developing Grounded Theory. *Sage*.

Te One, S. (2011). Defining rights: Children's rights in theory and in practice. *He Kupu, The Word, 2*(4), 41-57.

Te One, S., & Dalli, C. (2013). The status of children's rights in Early Childhood Education policy 2009. *New Zealand Annual Review of Education, 19*, 52-77.

Tesar, M. (2016). An overview of Childhood Studies. In: M.A. Peters (Ed.),s *Encyclopedia of Educational Philosophy and Theory* (A-F, pp. 261-267). Springer.
[http://dx.doi.org/10.1007/978-981-287-532-7_261-1]

Thomas, N. P. (2021). Child-led research, children's rights and Childhood Studies: A defence. *Childhood*, 1-14.
[http://dx.doi.org/10.1177/0907568221996743]

Troman, G. (1996). The Rise of the New Professionals? The restructuring of primary teachers' work and professionalism. *Br. J. Sociol. Educ., 17*(4), 473-487.
[http://dx.doi.org/10.1080/0142569960170404]

UN Committee on the Rights of the Child (CRC). (2001). *General Comment No. 1: Article 29(1): The aims of Education.* https://www.refworld.org/docid/4538834d2.html.

UN Committee on the Rights of the Child (CRC). (2005). *General Comment No. 7: Implementing Child Rights in Early Childhood, CRC/C/GC/7/Rev.1.* https://www.refworld.org/docid/460bc5a62.html.

UN Committee on the Rights of the Children (CRC). (2009). *General Comment No. 12 The right of the child to be heard.* https://www.refworld.org/ docid/4ae562c52.html.

UN Committee on the Rights of the Children (CRC). (2013). *General Comment No. 14 on the right of the child to have his or her best interests taken as a primary consideration (art. 3, para. 1).* https://www.refworld.org/docid/51a84b5e4.html.

UN Committee on the Rights of the Children (CRC). (2013). *General Comment No. 17 (2013) on the right of the child to rest, leisure, play, recreational activities, cultural life and the arts (art. 31)*.* https://www.refworld.org/docid/51ef9bcc4.html.

UN General Assembly. (1989). *Convention on the rights of the child.* https://www.refworld.org/docid/3ae6b38f0.html.

U.S Department of State. (2017). International Religious Freedom Reports: on International Religious Freedom: Greece. https://www.state.gov/reports/2017-report-on-international-religious-freedom/greece/

U.S Department of State. (2017). International Religious Freedom Report : United Kingdom.

References

https://www.state.gov/reports/2017-report-on-international-religious-freedom/united-kingdom/

Vasquez, V.M. (2004). *Negotiating critical literacies with young children.* Routledge.
[http://dx.doi.org/10.4324/9781410611109]

Verma, G.K., & Mallick, K. (2004). *Researching Education: Perspectives and techniques.* Falmer.

Vygotsky, L.S. (1966). Play and its role in the mental development of the child. *Voprosy psikhologii,* 12(6), 62-76.

Walkerdine, V. (1993). Beyond Developmentalism? *Theory Psychol.,* 3(4), 451-469.
[http://dx.doi.org/10.1177/0959354393034004]

Walkerdine, V. (1998). Developmental psychology and the child-centred pedagogy: The insertion of Piaget in early education. In: W. Hollway J. Henriques C. Venn C. Urwin & V. Walkerdine (Eds.), *Changing the subject: Psychology, social regulation and subjectivity* (pp. 153-202). Routledge.
[http://dx.doi.org/10.1177/0959354393034004]

Warner, L., & Lynch, S.A. (2004). *Preschool classroom management.* Gryphon House Inc..

Warren Little, J. (1993). Teachers' professional development in a climate of educational reform. *Educ. Eval. Policy Anal.,* 15(2), 129-151.

Warshak, R.A. (2003). Payoffs and pitfalls of listening to children. *Fam. Relat.,* 52(4), 373-384.
http://www.jstor.org/stable/3700318
[http://dx.doi.org/10.1111/j.1741-3729.2003.00373.x]

Wilson, V. (1997). Focus Groups: a useful qualitative method for educational research? *Br. Educ. Res. J.,* 23(2), 209-224.
[http://dx.doi.org/10.1080/0141192970230207]

Wood, E. (2010). Developing integrated pedagogical approaches to play and learning. In P. Broadhead J. Howard & E. Wood (Eds.), *Play and Learning in the Early Years* (pp. 9-26). Sage.

Wood, E., & Attfield, J. (1996). *Play, learning and the early childhood curriculum.* Paul Chapman.

Woodhead, M. (1999). Reconstructing Developmental Psychology - Some first steps. *Childen & Society,* 13, 3-19.
[http://dx.doi.org/10.1111/j.1099-0860.1999.tb00097.x]

SUBJECT INDEX

A

Abuse 2, 9, 29, 30, 142, 151
  physical 142, 151
  sexual 29, 30
Abusive teacher 54
Access information 2, 49
Activities 55, 111, 113, 185, 150
  physical 55
  recreational 185
  teacher-directed 150
  teacher-led 111
  time 113
Adult(s) 2, 14, 15, 185
  gaze playgrounds 185
  life 14
  act 2, 14, 15
Agency, children's 6, 24, 39
Agents 6, 16
  social 6
Alarms, smoke 77
Animal's welfare 162
Anonymity 34, 35, 100, 171
  children's 34
Attire, children's 90, 181

B

Behavioristic technique 81
Behavior(s) 17, 18, 20, 21, 26, 28, 37, 40, 49, 56, 58, 60, 89, 122, 136, 138, 139, 151, 166, 184
  children's 89, 122
  communicative 40
  issues 184
  teacher's 122
  unacceptable 151
Bicycle 83, 136, 137, 148
  giant 136
Board 16, 87, 156, 159, 189
  diving 159
  games 16, 87, 156, 189
Books, reading 115, 184
Bouncy castles 55
Boxing sack 155
Bullying, avoiding 78

C

Care, animal 166
Castle, bouncing 47
Change school cultures 23
Chenille stem 72
Child 14, 17, 28, 51, 54, 86, 93, 111, 150, 184, 188
  apologise 51
  behavior 14
  development 14
  initiated activities 28, 54, 86, 111, 150, 184, 188
  relationships 93
  sociologist 17
Children 4, 8, 7, 12, 13, 14, 15, 16, 19, 33, 51, 56, 63, 86, 89, 94, 98, 102, 11, 113, 142, 143, 146, 150, 152, 169, 173, 176, 179, 185, 186, 188
  agency 173
  activities 15
  complaining 169
  developing 102
  developmental stage 185
  dignity 51, 56, 98, 179
  education 12
  harming 94, 113
  health 188
  individualism and independence 15
  issues 19
  learning 14, 16, 102, 152
  naughty 89
  participation rights 14
  preparation 14, 111
  prioritize 33, 176
  protecting 146
  punishes 70, 183

relieve 36
resources 79, 89, 176
restrained 169
rights 8, 78
school layouts 146
scold 51, 142
sinner 13
tasks 150
teaching 63, 86
thinking 89
transitioning 185
younger 4, 143
youngest 7, 185, 186
Children's 4, 5, 14, 18, 19, 20, 21, 27, 49, 72, 76, 81, 89, 99, 105, 107, 146, 158, 167, 174, 187
  cooperation 187
  disputes 19
  education 14, 21, 158, 174
  learning and development 5
  minds 107
  perceptions, young 18, 72
  protection 4
  safety 49, 76, 81, 89, 99, 105, 146
  sleepovers 167
  tasks 20
  thoughts 27
Children's rights 23, 24, 28, 175
  implementing 23, 28
  young 24, 175
Chocolate 130, 133
  cake 130
  fountain 130
  lollipop 133
Circle time 18, 69, 86, 107, 147, 149, 155
  activity 18
  area 69, 107, 147, 149, 155
  carpet 86
Classes 36, 66, 188
  nursery 36, 66
  primary 188
Classmates 32, 49, 73, 94, 122, 124, 151, 157, 167, 170, 171
  stories 157
Classroom 13, 26, 45, 46, 53, 59, 63, 65, 66, 67, 68, 77, 85, 86, 87, 88, 89, 93, 112, 116, 121, 124, 126, 137, 138, 143, 147, 164, 165, 166, 168, 170
  decorated 164
  dialogue 26

environment 89
larger 65
layout 147
organization 86
pets 53
rules 59, 63, 66, 112, 116, 121, 124, 126, 137, 138, 166, 168, 170
walls 124
Clown 84, 153
Community, social 40
Connotations, negative 10
Corners, pastry shop 110
Cultures 2, 9, 10, 20, 21, 23, 24, 28, 29, 30, 39, 40, 174, 175
  children's 2
  dominant 21, 23, 40
  societal 28
  teacher's 23, 175
Cup cakes 165

D

Desks 13, 29, 30, 42, 74, 84, 88, 89
  rows of 13, 29, 30, 42, 74, 84
  teacher's 88, 89
Destructive nature 184
Development 2, 5, 6, 14, 15, 40, 109, 111, 178, 185, 187, 188
  human 185
  intellectual 185
  professional 188
Developmental 9, 185
  level 9
  psychology and early childhood education 185
Developmental psychology 12, 14, 17, 28, 35, 74, 75, 77, 79, 81, 83, 85, 87, 89, 91, 93, 95, 97, 99, 147
  school based on traditional 12, 14, 17, 28, 147
Diet, healthy 188
Differences 7, 21
  economic 21
  respect for 7
Dignity 3, 6, 13, 14, 16, 38, 51, 98, 124, 152
  children's 3, 152
  human 38
Dimensions, cultural 21, 174
Dinosaurs, flying 153
Discrimination, racial 7

Disobedience 51, 93
  children's 51
Disobeyed rules 51
Duties, teacher's 118

E

Early childhood education 8, 17, 185
Echo article, children misbehavior 51
Education 2, 3, 4, 6, 7, 8, 10, 11, 13, 14, 21, 22, 24, 28, 34, 37, 38, 55, 59, 72, 73, 84, 87, 91, 124, 126, 128, 134, 154, 166, 173, 174, 186, 188, 189
  adult directed 22, 174
  child-centered 11, 154
  compulsory 72, 73
  friendly 134
  human rights 91
  official 24, 38
  philosophy 28
  preschool 6, 34
  provisions 37, 188
  secondary 3
  systems 21, 24, 37, 174, 186, 189
  teaching 84
Education policy 23, 113
  primary 113
Exploitation 4
  economic 4
  sexual 4
Expression 3, 7, 27, 74, 78, 178, 181
  freedom of 3, 7, 74, 78, 178, 181
  non-verbal 27

F

Food 95, 96, 102, 103, 125, 126, 128, 130, 131, 133, 134, 139, 146, 147, 150, 161, 163, 165, 167, 168, 169, 170, 180, 181
  healthy 130, 139, 181
  spill 102
  sugary 180
  unhealthy 125, 126, 133, 134, 139, 146, 147, 161
Football playground 149
Free activity time 18
Freedom, children's 167
Fun fair 163, 172

G

Gray's definition 186
Gymnastics 102, 104

H

Hill school 66, 93, 99
  in Scotland 66
  rules 93, 99
Homework 92, 185
Hopscotch area 110
Horses 83, 84, 153, 162, 163
  little 163
  real 162
House 30, 31, 45, 50, 74, 80, 83, 101, 108, 110, 129, 162
  big green 80
  little 110

I

Ice 132, 165
  cubes 165
  lollies 132
Ice cream 81, 133
  fat 133
  giant 81
International humanitarian law 7

L

Language 3, 4, 7, 21, 25, 29, 37, 114, 187
  official 25
Learner's age 14
Learning 5, 6, 13, 15, 25, 76, 102, 105, 111, 114, 121, 132, 134, 138, 147, 154, 170, 180, 182, 183, 184
  academic 114, 138
  devalue 154
  difficulties 25
  equipment 183
  indoors 147
  materials 184
Linguistic minorities 4

Subject Index

M

Mobile phones 39
Moray house school 34
Mother tongues 30, 38
Motivation, intrinsic 187
Multiplicity 37
Museum 31, 101
Musical instruments 158

N

Natural environment 4, 7, 40, 44, 49, 54, 59, 63, 81, 84, 169
Nutrition, healthy 121, 134, 170, 180

O

Obstacle 75, 99, 102, 162, 163
    courses 75, 99, 102
    jumping 162
Outdoors, ground 110

P

Palm trees 81, 82
Parental permissions 34
Pastry shop 109, 110
    area 109
    label 110
Pencil case 123, 125
Playing 96, 97, 98, 182
    arrangements 96
    football 97, 98
    indoors 182
Playschool teacher 19, 181, 182
Political opinion 3
Primary education 3, 24, 92, 175
  child-centered 24, 175
Puppies, younger 143
Puzzles 52, 53, 87, 108, 150, 152

R

Raspberries, people blowing 137
Research, conduct emancipatory 18

Resources 28, 44, 49, 55, 86, 102, 111, 124, 131, 138, 149, 150, 152, 158, 176, 177, 183, 185
  entertainment 158
  material 185
Right to education 42, 44, 74, 101, 121, 127
Role, teacher's 19, 49, 94, 147, 170
Rooms 30, 74, 84, 134
  giant 134
  large 30, 74, 84
Rules 56, 57, 58, 68, 59, 60, 63, 66, 68, 98, 99, 70, 71, 93, 97, 112, 113, 120, 149, 151, 157, 166, 168, 169, 170, 171, 179, 180, 182
  bad 59, 60
  behavior 58, 149
  break 99
  class 60
  crazy 171
  lax 180
  linked 98
  safety 98
  silly 182
  strict 169, 180

S

School 4, 17, 18, 21, 22, 23, 25, 28, 29, 30, 31, 33, 36, 63, 65, 66, 71, 78, 79, 81, 90, 91, 99, 101, 112, 113, 115, 118, 128, 142, 161, 166, 175, 176, 178, 180, 183, 184
  children 23, 118, 175
  cultures 22, 23
  layout 142, 161
  library 72
  life 4, 91, 166
  matters 25, 91, 115, 183, 184
  nursery 36, 128
  paint 65
  play-based 180
  plans 33, 66, 176, 178
  policies 23, 113
  practices 17, 18, 28
  problems 31, 101
  provision 18, 21, 33, 176
  right-based 30
  royal 78, 79, 81
  rules 63, 71, 81, 112, 180, 183
  sessions 99

shortcomings 65
spacious 28
teach children 22
teacher-centered 29, 81, 90
Scolding 50, 51, 152, 161
  teacher's 50
Skills 102, 109
  children's motor 109
  physical 102
  social 102
Social 6, 15
    actors, young 6
    order 15
Society, multi-ethnic 24
Space, physical 49
Stereotypes 146

T

Tables, glittery 47
Teacher(s) 23, 28, 31, 56, 58, 60, 63, 64, 70, 71, 93, 94, 96, 98, 99, 115, 118, 120, 124, 130, 131, 135, 137, 139, 141, 142, 143, 146, 151, 152, 154, 157, 160, 168, 170, 179
  funny 139
  good 141, 142, 154
  head 93, 94
  ideal 137, 141, 160
  lady 143
  nice 124, 130, 135
  perfect 70, 152, 160, 168, 170
  primary 131
  silly 135
  strict 71, 137, 157, 168, 170
  wolf 143
Time 13, 19, 24, 28, 29, 31, 36, 43, 55, 56, 57, 58, 61, 70, 81, 94, 113, 114, 131, 132, 137, 161, 163, 177
  break 43
  disco 131, 137
  free 163
  golden 132
  spending 36
  tea 161
Toilets indoors 137
Tolerance 4, 7, 124, 149, 167
Tools 27, 72, 87, 107, 156
  magic 27

Toys 52, 53, 54, 55, 61, 64, 67, 83, 85, 105, 109, 126, 129, 140, 145, 147, 149, 150, 158, 159, 162
  big inflatable 83
  bombs 109
  cars 162
  fish 158
  fruit 55
  guns 109
  kitchen 53, 149, 162
  knives 105
  motorcycles 85
  pastry shop 110
  lots of 125, 129, 134, 149
  shop 162
  spiderman 153
  spiders 84
  sweets 110
  tools 55
  trucks 84, 85
  weapons 109
Traditional developmental psychology 12, 14, 17, 28, 38, 147, 185

V

Voice, children's 24, 25

W

Watch 32, 48, 122, 125, 155
  children's programs 155
  TV 32, 48, 122, 125
Water 39, 77, 80, 113, 123, 125, 130, 133, 137, 158, 159, 162
  bottles 113, 123, 125
  clean 39
  drink 159
  fights 80, 133, 137
  fountain 130
  pistols 80, 133
  spray 77

www.ingramcontent.com/pod-product-compliance
Lightning Source LLC
Chambersburg PA
CBHW042130010526
44111CB00031B/45